This book is dedicated to my wise and beautiful friend, Elizabeth Najda, who scolded me for pursuing the women and good times in Palm Beach. "Stop wasting your life, stay home and write," she said.

Unfortunately, researching my book created a conflict; occasionally I did have to slip back into the Palm Beach scene, strictly for research.

I am also grateful to my cousin, Ann Whittier, and Book Doctor Martine Bellin for their help editing, encouraging and just plain making sense of my scribbles.

Finally, many thanks to my close friend and best-selling author Marcia Chellis Kay for her weekly guidance and encouragement.

# Chapter 1

When Frank called, his usual inquiry about the raw Boston weather, followed by, "It's eighty-five here and not a cloud in the sky," was replaced by a straight-forward, "Tony, are you involved in a case?" Then, before I could reply, "I need your help," his voice, normally deep and deliberate, sounded uncharacteristically shaken.

"What's wrong Frankie?"

"Tony, I should know better. I got into one of those deals where they finance the purchase of an insurance policy on your life, hold it for two years, and then resell it to the highest bidder. My policy was just sold."

"How much insurance Frank?"

"Four million."

"Who bought it?"

"I don't know, but two guys that signed on to the same deal just before I did have shown up in the obituaries."

"Accidents?"

"No, heart stuff."

"Maybe a coincidence."

I was between cases and considering a vacation. Why not Palm Beach?

I wanted to ask Frank why he ever got into this crazy deal, but held my tongue. He needed help, not questions.

"I'll book a flight. Be there tomorrow."

I was familiar with the concept. Brokers lend elderly people money to buy an insurance policy. The insured keeps the policy for two years and has free coverage. After the two year holding period, when claims may be contested, the insured can pay back the loan with interest and keep the policy, or the broker sells it on the open market. Typically policies sell for a fat profit over the loan payments. This profit is split with the insured. Two years free coverage and a check at the end is hard to resist, but always raises that dark question: "Who will benefit from my death?"

Frank was approaching eighty, but a young eighty. He definitely wasn't planning on checking out this soon.

His call came on a Friday night. By mid-afternoon on Saturday I was sitting in first class on Jet Blue scheduled to land in West Palm International at 4:16.

I'm an insurance investigator and have Frank to thank for my profession.

He got me my first case with a wealthy Palm Beach matron, Harriet Fisher. Her long-time chauffeur had managed to insure her life without her knowledge. Five million bucks would provide his retirement a bit of the lifestyle he'd come to covet.

The chauffeur had discovered that his employer's doctor and lawyer were in cahoots with her heirs. Her step-children had lifestyles that outspent their trust income and were anxious for the big hit when Mrs. Fisher died. A couple of them decided to speed up God's process. They fired her longtime doctor and brought in their own guy, who turned a blind eye. Then they introduced a remedy used by women in seventeenth century Naples to rid themselves of abusive or boring husbands: A mixture of arsenic neutral salts, water, and the herb *Ranunculus* cymbalaria. A few drops added daily to soups, tea, or her favorite hot chocolate would cause a gradual loss of appetite, faintness, and eventual death. With the heirs help, the chauffeur found it easy to get the signatures and medical records needed to place insurance on her life.

They were very happy to include him. If anyone suspected foul play, his being the beneficiary of a life insurance policy would make him the prime suspect.

But there was a glitch. After he got the policy, the chauffeur found it contained a little clause called an incontestable period, which stated that if Mrs. Fisher died within two years, the company would review the medical records and have a right to contest a claim. This created a conflict. He needed her to live two years. The heirs were broke and wanted her dead sooner.

It got messy, as it always does when too many greedy people are involved. Then, when one of the adult grandchildren with a real job came to visit, he wondered why his "favorite Grammy" seemed to be sicker after the doctor left than before. This honest and loving grandchild knew Frank, who recommended me.

A background check revealed that the nephew who had instigated the plot had a gambling problem. I brought in another doctor and they were exposed.

The insurance company wanted to cancel the policy, and was within their rights to do so, but Mrs. Fisher, having been so close to death, suddenly liked the idea of insurance and decided to keep it. By updating the medical records, which showed her to be otherwise quite healthy, the issue was easily resolved. As soon as the poison was flushed from Mrs. Fisher's system, she got coverage. Fortunately, it was with a quality mutual company, and now, fifteen years later, the policy is paying for itself with dividends. One of her favorite charities will one day be five million richer.

The publicity of that first case taught a lot of heirs to be patient, but got some others thinking "outside the box." As referrals to other prominent families came my way, I learned about a thriving Palm Beach business: Doctors and lawyers, for the right price, will prove that a wealthy parent or grandparent is incompetent, so impatient heirs can gain control of their inheritance a little sooner.

Palm Beach, in many ways, fits Somerset Maugham's description of the South of France: "A sunny place for shady people."

Where there is wealth, there are scallywags.

This, of course, is what keeps me in business.

# Chapter 2

When you fly into West Palm and drive the few miles to the barrier island that is Palm Beach, signs of wealth are everywhere. On the way, you pass the large Jaguar, Lotus and Aston Martin dealerships. Bentleys and Rolls Royces are a dime a dozen. My rental, a cheap little 600 SL, had come from the Mercedes dealer two miles out on Okeechobee.

When I crossed the middle bridge, I could see the marina with dozens of multimillion dollar yachts. I tried to check the stern of what looked like Trump's new yacht to see if he had renamed it after his current wife, Melania. I couldn't tell.

Just over the bridge, on the lawn of The Four Arts Museum, sits the 12-meter yacht, America3, which billionaire Bill Koch funded and raced to bring the America's Cup back from Australia in 1995. It advertises his maritime collection on display at the museum.

The bridge empties onto Royal Palm Way, a divided road with a statue of, surprisingly, someone other than Henry Flagler, and three blocks of tall, stately palms. In those three blocks you pass Bank of America, U.S. Trust, Citibank, UBS, Atlantic Trust, Morgan Stanley, Lehman Brothers, Wachovia, Legg Mason, and others, all scrambling to "serve" this little town of 8,000 full-time residents. Henry Flagler's name is everywhere. The legal brains behind John

D. Rockefeller's monopoly of the oil industry, Flagler built a rail-road the full length of Florida's east coast, from the Georgia border to the southern-most tip of Key West. His trains allowed agriculture and tourism to develop as the state's two major industries. The crown jewel of the line, and his winter retreat, Palm Beach soon became a destination resort for the wealthiest families in America.

Even today, the town and the mix of people are still poles apart from where I grew up in Boston's North End, with its Italian restaurants, Catholic festivals, and three-generations of families living under one roof. From grade school through my college days, my mother's kitchen was filled with hearty smells, bubbling pots, my hungry friends, and my mother, with a pointed finger, dispensing advice on the world from her perspective as a Democratic ward boss.

My grandfather, my hero, was a detective on the Boston police force. I'd have been one too, but the odds of a smart-ass kid from Harvard making it on the Boston police force were somewhere between slim and none, regardless of who his grandfather might be.

My first taste of Palm Beach was spring break at the winter home of a Harvard classmate. It was delicious. I fell in love and eventually married his sister, Elizabeth. The spring visits to her family's winter estate continued until the divorce. Often, what attracts people from, in our case, very different backgrounds, can eventually be what creates a split. It was not bitter, just sad. We'd spent ten years being in love with what society judged to be the wrong person.

Her family was another reason I didn't follow my grandfather onto the police force. Selling life insurance was bad enough to them; a cop was on the same level as their help.

After the divorce, a few years passed until that first job, as a life insurance investigator for Mrs. Fisher, made Palm Beach a regular destination again.

# Chapter 3

I had booked a room for an indefinite stay at up the upscale Brazilian Court. Fortunately for me, my second career as an insurance detective pays well. It requires an insider's knowledge of insurance companies and products, which my fifteen years in sales and management provided, a strong dose of chutzpah, which growing in Boston's Italian North End provided, and the ability to know which to use when, which my Harvard education supplied.

My work is with law firms whose clients have been mistreated by brokers or insurance companies, and for the companies themselves if they are being scammed on claims. My hourly rate makes the attorneys I work for flinch, but they pay it. I'm very good at what I do.

Frank's call couldn't have come at a more perfect time. I'd been involved for months in a complex case and needed some time off. Like the famous Breakers Hotel, the Brazilian is Palm Beach pricey, but if they're going to add twenty percent to my bill anyway, I prefer the more personal service of a small hotel. Brazilian Court, unlike many of the hotels here, is very intimate. It has a courtyard for breakfast and lunch that is Venice romantic. Don't let my job fool you. I love romantic.

Oh, another minor detail. There are, as they say, a plethora of single women in Palm Beach. They arrive for many reasons. Hazarding a guess would be like looking a gift horse in the mouth. To quote Frank, "Making a list of the reasons women come to Palm Beach is like returning home after 'trick or treating,' emptying your bag on the kitchen table, and attempting to count all the sweets. Why bother? Just enjoy."

The reasons are as diverse as the women. My male friends joke that women arrive here: just getting out of marriage, just getting into marriage, hoping to get into marriage, hoping to get out of marriage. Ask a woman what she's doing in Palm Beach and she'll say she's here for the wonderful weather, the shopping, the camaraderie of other women. Maybe it's just the chance to put on her nicest jewelry, get beautifully dressed, and go out alone or with others to fund-raising benefits, clubs, restaurants or the theater, all the while knowing it's the men, not women, who need to be married.

# Chapter 4

As I was unpacking in my east-side suite, I looked out to see the large courtyard, brimming with women in gowns and men in tuxedos. Charitable affairs are daily events in Palm Beach.

I took a quick shower to wash off the flight. While towel drying my hair, which is short enough to avoid a comb, I stood by the full length mirror. A little heredity and regular workouts has kept me in reasonable tone for a fifty-two-year-old. My square face makes for an easy shave, which allows me to get rid of my five o'clock shadow in the shower. I dressed quickly in a blazer, white slacks and open-collar blue striped shirt, and called the valet for my car. Frank and I were meeting for dinner and I was anxious to see my old friend and mentor.

As I got into the rental, I gave the kid a twenty. A good tip on the first day is always worth the money. I slipped in a South Pacific CD and cranked it up for "There is Nothing Like a Dame." The emotional rush that music can bring brought back thoughts of my mother, who had died after a long illness only six months earlier. My mother, God bless her, dragged my two brothers and me to Saturday matinees of the many shows that came to Boston's theater district. Her teenage dreams of a career in the theater were cut short by her marriage at twenty, the week my father went off to Korea. Maybe she wanted us to share her teenage dreams.

As I headed down Coconut Row, past the tall hedges that hide the estates from the road, I passed a gate which I recognized as leading to the estate of my first client and now friend, Harriet Fisher.

I pictured her Addison Mizner-designed home, built in the late 1920s by her patrician father-in-law. It's at the end of a long gravel driveway flanked by a thick green hedge. The hedge runs straight for two hundred yards due west toward the main house, and hides all but the roof of the two story gardener's cottage to the right of the electronically gated entrance. In the morning, the bedrooms on the east side receive streaks of pink and gold from behind the clouds that hover over the Breakers golf course. Except for sunrise and sunset, the road is shaded. The hedge opens to a row of evenly spaced palms allowing a view of the boxwood-rimmed gardens set up as octagons throughout the estate. Mr. Fisher was a math buff.

Mizner, a talented New York architect, came south in the early '20s, for his health. He brought his distinctive Moorish-Mediterranean architecture first to the Everglades Club, then to the grand estates of the Vanderbilts, Phippses, Morgans, and Fishers.

Beyond the row of palms, the drive splits around a large fountain with two nymphs bathing in a constant spray of water. The faded yellow home has a center section fronted by three large columns supporting a porte-cochere ("porch" to us plain folk) above the front door.

Typical of many Palm Beach homes, when you step inside you find you are still outside. An open courtyard forms the center section of the house, with marble walkways leading to sitting rooms, dining rooms, a library and an enormous kitchen. The wings stretch on forever, with balconies fronting the eight east-facing bedroom suites, each offering views of the gardens.

The west side of the house has a 3,000-square-foot ballroom

with eighteen-foot ceilings featuring six enormous chandeliers. The ceilings are covered by murals of clouds and angels. The dance hall opens to a large patio, then lawns sloping down to Lake Worth. A third floor above the center section contains the quarters for the staff of eight.

Like all Mizner homes, it features decorated concrete railings (balustrades). These front the balconies off each bedroom. Another feature of Mizner, still copied in homes built today, is the mix of rectangular windows on the north side and arched windows on the south.

As I drove by, I thought about that kind woman living there for years, knowing that the step-grandchildren she had supported had been involved in or turned a blind eye in the plot to take her money and sell this beautiful estate. The good news was that local charities for kids were now doing quite well with some of the money once anticipated by those who had plotted against her.

I decided to call on her later in the week, but I first had to focus on Frank. When Helene, Frank's wife, had died a year ago, I was chasing down a case in Europe. Instead of acknowledging our long friendship, putting life in perspective, and flying back for the funeral, I stayed in Europe. Maybe with my mother's illness I couldn't face Helene's death. Who knows? His call brought back the guilt. Maybe this trip would bring redemption. I had met all three of Frank's wives. He and his first wife, whom I'd met after their divorce, had gradually grown apart. That early physical heat was long gone, and though a mutual respect remained, it wasn't enough for Frank. The long hours spent building a business, combined with the joy of raising two daughters, kept them together until Frank was in his mid 40's. They separated amicably when his girls were still in college.

He was tall and lean with broad shoulders that gave him the

look of an attractive Abe Lincoln. An easy smile and quick wit made him a favorite with the ladies, but like many of us men, he often made the mistake of confusing lust and love. The woman he was lusting after at the time mistook his lust for love. For Frank, an honorable man, this resulted in his ill-fated second marriage. He waited many years to try again. The third time it was love matching love. He and Helene were a perfect fit.

I pictured him ten years ago with his arm around his new wife, Helene, at their wedding in the Greek Orthodox Church in the village of Fira. The village stands a thousand feet above the Aegean, on the island of Santorini. Dozens of friends from Boston and Palm Beach had spent nearly a week celebrating the wedding. Helene was a brilliant pianist and an elegant lady.

They had been so in love. After two missteps, he'd finally found the perfect match for his high energy and passion for life. They had spent the next eight great years in Greece. Two years ago she had fallen victim to a rare form of cancer and had moved back to the States for her treatment. In spite of my visiting Palm Beach several times in the past two years, I had not seen them since the wedding.

Santorini's romantic views, villas cut into the cliffs, the endless night life, and gracious people made the week-long wedding unforgettable. But for me it was bittersweet. I thought I had met the love of my life and brought her to the wedding. She was a Russian with piercing blue eyes, pitch-black, waist-length hair, the softest pure white skin, and a passion that was unsurpassed. During our trip, she realized there were men from Palm Beach whose jewelry budgets had no limits, and I wasn't one of them. Maybe I should have been more guarded, moved more slowly, but that's not me. Nothing ventured, nothing gained. Always the romantic optimist, damn the torpedoes, full speed ahead. That's my style.

Frank has a presence, a self-confidence that together with his wit and high energy attracts people to him. I knew when he saw me through the crowd at the Palm Beach Grill he'd yell out, "Tony. Over here." Next, I'd get that warm smile and a hug. He'd order me a Dewar's and soda, and while waiting, out would come the pictures of his three grandchildren. They'd be frayed and torn at the edges from pushing them in and out of his wallet for anyone who would look and listen. Sophie, whom I had last seen at the wedding, was now sixteen and a knockout like her mother. Frank's first words when he saw his minutes-old granddaughter were, "That kid's so good-looking. She looks just like me." Frank was never shy, nor lacking humor.

The Grill is at the far end of a plaza, a complex of real estate offices and shops on the corner of Coconut Row and Royal Poinciana. It's across from the mandatory hedge hiding the 16th hole of the Breakers Golf Course.

Behind the Grill, on the inland waterway, is the old Poinciana Playhouse, where ever major actor from Helen Hayes on has played.

The Grill has been a happening place for some time, mainly in the early evening. You have to call Eddie a week ahead or more for a reservation in the dining room, and after about six-thirty it's a forty-five-minute wait at the bar. No one cares; the people-watching is first class. Since nearly everyone is from somewhere else, meeting new friends is easy. Prior to the present ownership, the grill was a late night spot, Au Bar. When you mention it, the typical comment is, "Oh, that's where Kennedy..."

Except for a charitable event at their home, or a photo to promote a favorite cause, most of the old money in Palm Beach remains invisible to the tourists.

In Palm Beach, as you might guess, there are palm trees every-where. I made a left turn into the Plaza and took a parking spot at the fifth palm. I walked past another fifteen to the heavy wooden door. The valet held it open with a smile and a "Good evening, sir."

I cringed at that "sir" bit. It makes me feel old. Of course, com-pared to the kid at the door, I am.

I excused my way through the crowd, to an opening at the left end of the L-shaped bar, where it was only two bodies deep. Dave, the bartender, handed me a Dewars and soda and pointed to Frank seated at the other end of the bar. He was somehow saving me a stool. When I finally made it through the crowd, Frank, still a few inches taller than my six feet, stood up, grabbed me by the shoulders, and gave me that famous hug. Time had added a few wrinkles, but as always, he stood straight as a rod with his grip still surprisingly firm. My dad died when I was young. Frank, always available with advice and emotional support, had in some ways replaced him.

With hands on my shoulders, he said, "You haven't lost the good looks Tony." He leaned a little closer and added, "Cutting your hair short to cover that gray in the temples?"

Before I could reply with a defense, he continued, "It's been a long time."

"It has. Not since…" I stopped.

He finished, "My wedding to Helene." His head bent forward ever so slightly, his eyes looked down, and his voice trailed off.

We stood in silence for a moment. I'd been running through excuses on the drive over. Glib half truths are my specialty. "Sorry, I didn't make the funeral," was all I could muster.

"Wouldn't have brought her back."

Then he smiled and his blue eyes took on that familiar, let's live for today twinkle. As if by script, his next words were: "Let me show you my grandchildren." Sure as rain, out came the pictures, first Sophie, and then the two boys.

"Good-looking kids, Frank. They look just like you."

He smiled and slapped me on the back, acknowledging I'd stolen his line.

But now his smile was gone. "Tony, you got time to stay for awhile? I'm in a real bind." I nodded and waited for him to tell me what I already had guessed. "The thing is this, Tony. Without looking close at who I was really dealing with, I had them buy back the policy. I've got no wife to leave it to, and I've already set up trusts for my grandchildren. Didn't seem I needed it; plus, the interest they charged would make a loan shark blush. After the sale supposedly goes through, and I say supposedly because I've yet to see any of the big bucks promised, I'll get a check for about three hundred big ones."

He stopped, glanced behind him, and lowered his voice. "Now I hear from a reliable source that the guy who sold me the deal is working for some very bad people."

That tone from his Friday night call had returned.

I was concerned, but didn't want him to know it, so I tried to sound upbeat. "Frank, there is sleet, rain, and its thirty degrees in Boston. Palm Beach is seventy-five and sunny. There are more good-looking, sophisticated women per square foot here than anywhere in the country. No contest. I'm staying until my money runs out."

Frank laughed and waved to Rebecca, the bartender with the perfect smile. In her real life she's a cabaret singer on cruise ships. This job is a fill-in, until her agent gets her a new gig.

I didn't mention to Frank that I had called Sonja as soon as I got off the plane. Sonja is a combination package of Latin descent, with the best from every country involved. We've been friends since her first year with the Palm Beach Police. She pulled me over for speeding and I showed her my grandfather's Boston Police detective badge. She smiled, shook her head, and handed it back with the ticket. The next morning I saw her in Green's. She recognized me and asked if that badge trick ever worked. We both had a chuckle and hit it off from the start. I was working on the Fisher case, and she turned out to be a great source for local knowledge and contacts. In return, I have also been of help to her; I have a few less rules (think none) governing what I can and cannot do.

She wasn't aware of this insurance syndicate but said she'd look into it. She also said her husband was being squeezed out of his job at a local firm whose parent company is in Boston. She hoped I might know someone there. We planned to meet.

There are two large rectangular mirrors behind the bar at the Grill. You can see most of what's going on in the entire room without turning your head. Frank and Rebecca were discussing the Dover sole special. I was watching a brunette. Her face was turned toward her friend. My eyes were slowly following the line of her bare shoulder, down to her smooth, tanned arm. I stopped at the bent elbow to enjoy her narrow waist, then started up again past two plain gold bracelets, and on to the long thin fingers playing with her hair. No ring. There was a sensuousness and class in this well-groomed woman's hands.

To my left, a slightly overweight blonde with a nose too close to her upper lip, wearing a dress she'd obviously bought before she had gained weight, had been carrying on a one-way conversation about the hot real estate market. While tracking the mystery woman, I had been nodding with an occasional yes at her seemingly innocent chatter. Suddenly her card appeared. Michelle something, real estate. Dave the bartender, who had been watching this Michelle woman work me, was sporting a big smile. He rolled his eyes, while shaking his head and mouthing the word NO.

I said, "Thank you, I'm not in the market."

She gave me a dirty look as if to say, "Why have I wasted my time?" and got up and left.

Dave leaned on the bar in front of me. "Last week she was having a similar conversation with a gentleman having dinner at the bar. He made the mistake of telling her that he might be selling his house. He got home an hour later to find her swimming naked in his pool." He smiled and pointed his finger. "It's a competitive market down here."

Frank was telling Rebecca a story. She was laughing.

"Same old Frank," I thought. A little less hair, a few more lines around the eyes. But his appreciation of life hadn't changed.

Rebecca headed for the open kitchen next to the bar to put in the order. The smells and controlled chaos reminded me of my mother's kitchen, when she would be cooking and carrying on conversations with three people at once. I pictured her stirring sauce while talking to my grandfather, our neighborhood priest, Father Crowley, and some political crony.

I missed her. Hopefully all those meals she fed Father Crowley helped her to a better place. I thought about how similar Helene's illness and passing were to my mother's.

Frank, who was watching Rebecca in the kitchen, turned back to me. "I ordered you the ribs. This place has the best."

He gave me another pat on the back. "Thanks for coming down. Let me tell you the latest."

I tried to focus on Frank, not the mirror.

He began, "A friend of mine, who recently became terminally

ill, had bought the same deal I did. In fact, I first heard about it from him. He called me, knew I'd been in the business. Anyway, a few years go by, now they're after him to sell his policy, but he's decided to keep it. He's gonna die, so of course he should keep it. But guess what? He tells me this guy who sold it to him is making not so subtle threats that he'd better sell.

So I say, 'What do you mean not so subtle?' And he says, 'We really want your policy,' and then starts asking about my friend's grandchildren."

"Frank, this isn't like you. How'd you get involved in this deal anyway?"

"Well, a little more than two years ago, I'm looking for something to kill an afternoon. Helene was at the hospital taking some tests. So I go to a seminar on estate planning. Old clients sometimes call. I like to keep up."

He paused, held up his wine glass. He took a sip, and smiled. "This place is like nowhere else. There are seminars every day telling you how to manage your money, and there's a charity ball every night asking you to give it away. On the way to the seminar or fund-raiser you can turn on the radio and hear about vitamins and herbs to keep you alive, and the next station will tell you how to get to heaven if the vitamins don't work."

"So anyway," Frank continued, "There were a couple of attorneys discussing ideas for avoiding death taxes, and this guy Ryan giving his spiel about this life insurance plan. I spoke with him afterward, more out of curiosity than anything. Insuring people and then selling the policies" Frank shook his head. "Things sure have changed since I left the business."

Frank could tell by my expression I still didn't understand why he got involved.

He shrugged and continued. "At first I wasn't that interested, but Ryan gave me the names of a few people who had bought. I knew one of them and called him. He said his attorneys had checked it out. It was legit. Helene had just been diagnosed with a rare of type of cancer. They felt she'd survive, but it would take time. She has no relatives in the States. I was concerned for her. I thought why not? Free insurance and a check at the end, what did I have to lose? Talk about being dead wrong. I'm worried. I gave them control of the policy. Who'd they sell it to? Some hit man for a piece of the four mill? You know as well as I do, Tony, a lot of wise guys come to Boca. Just because they're on vacation and enjoying the sun with their bimbos, doesn't mean they would turn down a little business."

I glanced in the mirror at the brunette with the sweet hands. She was three quarters facing me now, gesturing to her friend. There was something European in her manner, maybe the exaggerated motion of her hands.

Frank continued, "How can a company sell me a policy so cheap that I can resell it and make a profit?"

The intensity of her conversation allowed me to watch without being seen. She had large brown eyes, set wide apart, with thick brows and long lashes, and a small upturned nose. Her lips were full, with the upper lip slightly more prominent, creating the appearance of a pout. Her smile, which seemed her natural expression, created the slightest hint of lines in her smooth olive skin. She stood very erect and balanced, like an athlete ready to spring. Her dress, which stopped just below the knee, was cherry red, smooth like satin, and tight enough to stir my fantasies.

Frank had been talking, but I was only half listening.

"Get focused, Tony. I'll introduce you to the brunette later."

Good old Frank, always knew what I was thinking, not that he had to be a mind reader.

"Companies want to own policies on older people because they die sooner," I told him.

Frank smiled and started to say something. But I continued, "Seriously, because the service is so poor and the business so cutthroat, most policies are dropped or replaced for a new commission. These companies sell you a policy and hope you don't keep it. They have been under pricing policies for years knowing most are dropped before they ever pay a claim."

I snuck a glance at the brunette and continued. "Now other companies get wise and started buying these under priced policies. Just a matter of time before they start looking for people to insure to create their own inventory. Give me the guy's card."

I read the name, Timothy Ryan, President of Life Concepts, 2238 Belvedere, Suite 4, West Palm Beach.

I held up the card. "I'll pay him a visit when he's not there."

Frank smiled, "Sounds like a plan; tomorrow's Sunday." He added, "It's a new single-story building on the right, just before Route 95."

He put his hand on my shoulder and gave it a squeeze. "Thanks."

I could see her face in the mirror now. She was laughing at something her friend had said. She seemed so comfortable, so self-assured. Everything she did appeared so natural, so free. Her girlfriend spotted me watching them in the mirror. They seemed to know Frank. Maybe they were trying to figure what we were discussing so intently in a place where people just had fun.

I wondered if her friend had told her I was staring. I turned on my stool to look directly at her. I guess she had. When I looked, she stared back and didn't turn away until a hint of a smile let me know she'd been watching me too. That's European. They don't do that in Boston.

I'm maybe too selective as to what I like, so sometimes I'm a little surprised when the woman returns the interest. I'm decent-looking, but women's taste in men is as varied as the women. You look and smile and spin the dial.

I realized Frank was saying something. "Be careful Tony. I don't know if it's Ryan or the people he represents, but there are some bad people involved in this."

I tried to focus on Frank. "Sunday office visits are much more relaxed. I can poke around and not be bothered."

I put my arm around his shoulder and gave him a reassuring hug. The hug was real, but I also wanted the pretty brunette to know we were close.

"It seems there've been threats, but they apparently have insured quite a few people. No one has been killed yet."

Frank seemed to buy it, but I was worried. If the wrong people owned his policy, he could be in trouble.

"I'd appreciate anything you can dig up, Tony. I'm too old to deal with this stuff."

The crowd at the bar was moving behind me. I'd feel an occasional bump and an "excuse me."

I was trying to focus when I felt the lightest touch of a woman's fingertips across my back and in a woman's voice with a slight accent, a very soft "good night." Was it her? Was she speaking to me? I was facing Frank; I couldn't turn to look. All that remained was the slightest hint of cologne. Lavender?

I tried to refocus. "Life insurance is a wide-open business, Frank. The loose rules attract scum. Too bad, there are a lot of quality companies and agents, but the fringe is nasty."

"I know." He replied. "Not like the old days when guys were in it as a career. Now we've got too many stockbrokers and so-called financial planners selling policies with companies that only care about quarterly earnings. Too many attorneys are referring business to broker friends, regardless of the quality of their products."

I checked the mirror. The brunette and her friend were gone. Getting up quickly I headed for the door to see if she was waiting for her car. No luck.

When I got back, Frank had that knowing smile. "Another one gets away. You'll get another shot. She's in here on Fridays with her girlfriends. They leave here and go to the Colony to dance. She's a very educated woman, and may not be your type."

Frank knows I'm attracted to smart women and was trying to get a rise out of me.

I gave it back. "Not true, Frank. Once in a while I enjoy a woman with a brain. It's a nice change."

"I watched you look at her. Where you were looking was not where she keeps her brains."

"Too bad. Kill two birds with one stone."

Frank was now into his hard-luck-with-women bit. "You're lucky, you have that clean cut all-American look that women love. Me, the only luck I get is the hard kind. I'm going home to get some sleep. I'll buy you breakfast at Green's. 8:30?"

We walked out together. As I waited with Frank for his car, he put his arm around my shoulder and leaned close. "Tony, have you ever been to a bullfight?"

"No. Why?"

"There's a word for the moves the bullfighter uses to entice the bull to charge, to bring him close enough to excite the crowd, but not so close he gets gored. It's called *suertes*."

I smiled and nodded. He'd been paying closer attention to my moves with the mystery woman than I thought. The valet was waiting with his car. He took a step toward it, and then turned to face me. "The singular of the word, *suerte*, means luck."

I walked back to the car, past the real estate offices and rows of palms, and thought about how right Frank was. You can perfect all the moves you make to close a business deal, attract a woman, whatever, and luck often turns out to be the most important element.

I raced the big engine, put the top down and turned on a Ray Charles disc, "Georgia on My Mind."

Sitting alone in the warm star-filled night, I thought about Frank's "no luck with women" comment and smiled. Six guys could share his good times and all think they'd done just fine.

I thought about the brunette and about men watching women. I'm like a lot of guys. I look and look, and seldom act, unless the woman makes the first move. On a rare occasion, I find a woman so special, all bets are off. I pursue. Was this that woman?

Frank was smart enough to go home. I wasn't. I punched in a name on my cell.

Years ago, Kate and I had been an item back home, when things had gotten real messy at the tail end of my marriage. After my divorce we'd seen each other off and on for several years. But she was always busy with kids and jobs, and with no help from ex-husbands; our relationship evolved into a close friendship with great sex. She'd moved south a couple of years back when her kids left the nest. When I was in town for more than a couple of days, we usually hooked up. We had history that made it easy to connect and disconnect.

We also shared a little issue called commitment. We were a match made in heaven, but I put down the phone. I didn't want her to know I was in town. Not yet. Not until I'd found out about the brunette who stared back.

# Chapter 5

The next morning I awoke to that initial confusion of being in a strange place. It was still dark. The blinds and nearly floor-to-ceiling windows were partially opened to Palm Beach's warm salt breeze. Old Henry Flagler knew what he was doing. Thanks to the constant breeze, and being surrounded by salt water, there are few bugs.

Frank would kid, "We don't allow bugs in Palm Beach."

I was fully awake, so I pulled on my Seven jeans and Ralph Lauren jersey. I'd seen Kate a few months before; she'd insisted on the expensive jeans. "You're not in the North End. This is Palm Beach. Look the part," she'd said.

I decided to explore.

At the small bar in the center of the long narrow lobby was freshly brewed coffee in an ornate silver service that looked like a prize in a tennis tourney. I ignored the fancy china and found a Styrofoam cup behind the bar. The cheap cups keep the coffee warm longer.

Too early for the New York Times, I picked up a copy of Palm Beach Today, the weekly "society and lifestyle" newspaper.

I put my coffee on the side table and settled in on the couch. "Cancer Ball raises $2,143,400. Norton Museum's *Bal des Arts* raises $1,000,000 for special exhibits." And another bank opens in Palm Beach. Then pages of photos. Each event's chairpersons, major contributors, Rod Stewart dining with friends, photo after photo of be's and wannabe's.

I flipped through to the last few pages. Car ads, real estate ads, an advertisement by a dentist telling the benefits of having your mouth remodeled. Only $29,995. Such a deal!

Ever since the '30s, when Mrs. Merriweather Post built her 117-room mansion, Mara-a-Lago, and began flying in royalty and movie starts, charitable balls and benefits have been a way of life in Palm Beach. Any day of the winter season, the folks in Palm Beach attend brunches, lunches, afternoon teas, and swank black-tie soirees. They range from the parvenus earning their stripes to those who control family foundations. They give for love of a cause, for love of a good time, or maybe just to be noticed, but give they do, by the tens of millions.

The morning quiet was gradually interrupted by the stir from the other end of the lobby. Waiters and kitchen staff were showing up for the morning shift, most coming in from across the bridge.

Time to get to work. I picked up the phone by the bar. "Car for Mr. Tauck, room 17."

"Yes sir, Mr. T. I'll have it up front in a moment."

I smiled. Either he remembered the twenty dollar tip, or had taken the car for a test drive. It didn't matter. As a kid I'd have done both.

I gave him another twenty. Sometimes the kids at these places have a better handle on what goes on than the police. Sunday morning, the streets would be quiet. It was over an hour before I was to meet Frank, plenty of time to check out Tim Ryan's office.

# Chapter 6

Crossing the bridge from Palm Beach to sections of West Palm is like watching Cinderella at midnight. Royal Palm Way turns into Lakeview, and less than a dozen blocks south on Dixie, I pass boarded-up buildings, pawn shops, and vacant lots. In Palm Beach, barely a mile away, tiny lots, blocks from the water, sell in the millions.

In the center of West Palm, urban renewal is taking hold. Cranes and construction equipment are everywhere. The new high-rise condos are scooped up by speculators the week the project is announced. Over a thousand people a day are moving to Florida, and the Palm Beaches are getting their share. But a mile south, where I'm going, things haven't changed.

I take a right on Belvedere, heading west toward the airport. On my left is a parking lot for the Winn Dixie, Family Dollar, and Subway. No Neiman Marcus in this section. The large lot is deserted, except for a few older-model cars in the northwest corner, near the Kitten Club.

It's seven a.m. I wondered if anyone was still there enjoying the "live adult entertainment" advertised on the large faded sign.

The single-story office building was easy to spot. The exterior was a sickly yellow, but the hedge and potted ferns lining the walk to the front door told me someone was at least trying.

I pulled over to get my bearings. As expected, no one was out at this hour in an all-business neighborhood.

The building looked like it housed four offices, two on either side of the front door, and was more upscale than I'd expected this close to the Kitten Club. Ryan's card said Suite 4, which I guessed would be on the far right. The parking was beyond the building in the rear. I drove down a slight incline and parked under the window that I assumed was the office of Life Concepts. I slipped on a pair of gloves. Maybe something in Tim Ryan's office would give me a clue as to his motives or character.

The window was about six feet off the ground. I stood gingerly on the car fender, trying to avoid an expensive dent or scratch. The window was plenty wide and unlocked. Someone must have felt it was high enough off the ground to not lock it. I was quickly inside.

There was a couch to my left and a large desk to the right with two chairs for guests. The desk was clean, but for a photo of three men posing with golf clubs. The man in the middle was considerably shorter and broader than the other two. He had dark hair in a crew cut with a hairline that came to a point in the front. Must be Ryan, I thought. If I meet him, I'm going to recommend he let his hair grow; that widow's peak is not attractive.

The top drawer in the desk was locked, but with a little help from a letter opener, the lock sprang easily. It looked like someone had left in a hurry and jammed all their papers, pencils, pens, and notebooks into the locked drawer for the weekend. Probably late for his golf game. I scooped up the entire contents, heaped it on the desk and started sifting through, still not sure what I was looking for.

After examining each sheet of paper in detail, I found copies of what appeared to be a similar letter sent to dozens of Palm Beach residents. Each letter asked for a meeting, then described a particular asset the letter's recipient owned, enticing them to meet for specific advice. At first it seemed a person would be annoyed by a letter inferring the sender had personal information about them, but the bottom of the letter had a disclaimer with an additional hook: "This information was obtained from public records, of which you may wish to be made aware." It was risky, but an interesting approach. Some may be annoyed, but others would be curious and meet.

Under the sheaf of letters was a large envelope containing a computer disc and a printout from an investment management firm, Fairfield & Ellis Investments, LLC.

I pulled it out, sat back in Mr. Tim Ryan's chair and read with amazement.

Suddenly I heard what sounded like a door slam.

I grabbed the stack of letters, stuffed the disc and computer sheets into the envelope, and ran to the open window. The morning air was calm. I had no choice. I dropped the entire stack of papers between the car and the building, hoping they wouldn't blow away. I scrambled out the window, trying to hold my footing on the car fender. As I slid backwards out the window I managed to pull it shut, just as I slid off the trunk. I scooped up the papers and threw them through the window into the passenger seat, expecting at any moment to see a head emerge from the window I had abruptly left.

I backed up the car to face the street. If someone was coming around from the front on foot, I could drive straight out and take a hard right away from the building. The entrance to Route 95 was a hundred yards away. This little rental could outrun anything a person in this neighborhood owned.

I drove out at a modest speed and, just in case anyone was looking, turned south on 95. The papers were blowing around on the seat. I pressed the button to roll up the windows.

I checked the mirror, saw no one had followed me, slowed down and pulled into the right lane. I turned east on Southern Boulevard and circled back across the Southern bridge into south Palm Beach. From there I headed north past Mar-a-lago and several miles of mansions before turning left at the Estee Lauder estate, which backs up to the Breakers Hotel. The homes on this stretch across from the beach are all fronted by walls and hedges. They're slightly smaller than Mrs. Fisher's estate and closer to the road. At the eastern end there are tunnels under the road to the ocean and, to the west, lots run all the way back to the lake. This is major-league money. Twenty rooms is small. Most are occupied maybe six weeks a year.

It was close to 8:30. At most, I'd be a couple of minutes late for breakfast with Frank.

# Chapter 7

The parking lot for Green's Pharmacy is on Sunrise, across North County Road from St. Edward's Catholic Church.

The lot was nearly full with the cars of early churchgoers, whose second Sunday ritual is breakfast at Green's.

Green's is a trip back in time. No more than a little paint on the walls has been added since the '60s, when Jack Kennedy had his Palm Beach White House at the family compound, about two miles north. There's a long counter with about twenty bar stools, open only for a few feet in the center. Waitresses squeeze hurriedly past one another to get to the toaster, coffee canister, or waffle iron, or to pick up orders yelled out by Shaun at the command post in the center of the action. "Carrie, Julie, Pattie. Order up." Shaun, cooking eight things at once, kidding with the girls, and all the while talking fishing with a couple of Palm Beach's finest. "Jackie. Order up!"

It's "hurry up and wait" for the girls at Green's as the crowd ebbs and flows with the hourly Masses at St. Edward's. Sunday is busiest, but the church gets a pretty good play every day. The bishop, who grew up in Brooklyn, knows enough to send the best priests to where the money is. The average age in Palm Beach being late sixties doesn't hurt attendance either.

It was too crowded to enter the restaurant at the back end, so I cut through the first aisle on the pharmacy side. Obviously devoted to the beach, one side holds goggles, blow-up rafts, and plastic surfboards. The other has every flavor of sun block you can imagine, and, in case you forget to use it, there is a small section for treating sunburn.

Frank was sharing a table with two women. He stood to greet me.

"Tony, I'd like you to meet my friends, Barbara Mallory and her daughter Daisy."

A remarkably well-preserved, attractive woman, dressed in a flowered hat and head-to-toe Chanel, stuck out her hand and smiled.

"Hello, Tony."

Daisy's slight nod, downcast eyes, lips that barely managed a smile, and no handshake, made it clear an Italian named Tony wasn't going to be included among her list of playmates.

I wasn't offended. As Frank would say, "Not everyone in the 'upper class' is."

Sensing the daughter's snub, Frank decided to up the ante.

He gave me a wink. "I know Tony through his Uncle Sal. Sal is vice chairman of Ferrari. We practically grew up together. How's Uncle Sal, Tony?"

I played along. "I just spoke to him yesterday; he's doing great. He's all excited, Maria's pregnant. They're hoping for a girl."

With the mention of Ferrari, Daisy sat up a little straighter and almost smiled.

"Oh, how nice," said Barbara, "a granddaughter."

I felt guilty misleading this very pleasant woman, "No, a daughter."

Barbara, the perfect lady, said, "I'm sorry, I guess I'm so envious of anyone who has grandchildren."

Daisy, clearly the expected bearer of the grandchildren, shifted her slim hips uncomfortably in her plastic chair.

She finally spoke. "Just how old is Uncle Sal?"

Frank gave her his best coy smile. "He's my age, Daisy, and at that you'll just have to guess."

Barbara, obviously enchanted by Frank, reached across the table and took his hand. "You don't know this, Tony, but I introduced Frank to Helena. She was a wonderful dancer. He brags about being the best dancer in Palm Beach. She taught him how. As for age, it's all in your head. Frank and I will be young forever."

We laughed. I decided to be a detective again. "Say Barbara, Uncle Sal asked me about an investment firm here in Palm Beach, Fairfield & Ellis."

"Oh, my goodness," said Barbara, "we know them well. My late husband used them for years. They are the investment arm of Bingham, Burroughs, DuPont, the oldest and most respected law firm in the area. They practically came down with Henry."

She smiled, and added without the slightest hint of pretence, "Henry Flagler."

The papers in my car just became a little more interesting, but I didn't want her to suggest an introduction, at least not until I talked with Frank.

I was saved. Nancy, our waitress, was holding two pots of coffee.

She smiled at Frank. "Coffee, tea, or me?"

"There are ladies present, Nancy. I'll have to settle for coffee, high test please."

Daisy frowned.

Barbara held out her cup. "A refill of the high-test for me, Nancy, and thank you, dear."

Suddenly, there was a clamor and a thud at the far end of the restaurant. A well-dressed gentleman sitting on the bar stool had slid off as he spun around to face the counter. He was getting to his feet, embarrassed, but uninjured.

Nancy, with a straight face, said, "People forget these are bar stools. Either that or he couldn't remember where his ass was."

Barbara was laughing with Nancy. Hopefully, she'd forgotten about investments. I had to wonder how a woman who was all class and no pretense could have bred such a stiff-ass for a daughter.

Nancy runs the hard-working waitress crew more by example than dictate. Her casual smile conceals that sharp tongue, which is accompanied by a husky laugh. The years of hard work and cigarette breaks only partially disguise a face and slim figure that, I'm certain, look better than good when she's out being served, instead of serving.

Frank had picked up on my Fairfield & Ellis quip, and was giving me a quizzical look. He put a twenty next to the ten-dollar check, and stood up.

"Tony and I need to take a walk. It's so nice to see you again, Barbara. Thank you for letting me join you two."

As expected, Barbara smiled and Daisy didn't.

I followed Frank out the back door.

I pointed to my car in the last row in the lot. "Let's go to my car. Maybe you can make some sense of this stuff I picked up from your friend Tim Ryan."

# Chapter 8

I got in and leaned over to push open the door for Frank. I held the papers until he got seated, and then passed them and waited for a response. The first page was stamped "Confidential" with the heading Bingham, Burroughs, DuPont.

Frank, not big on swearing, was clearly mouthing the Lord's name in vain. Finally he turned to face me. "Where did you get this stuff? Tim Ryan's office?"

He was asking and answering his own questions. Something he did often.

I nodded four times, and watched as he flipped through the computer runs. He would stop, I guessed, to read more detail on someone he knew, and then continue. Nowhere near halfway through, he stopped and stared at the papers on his lap.

"This gives the financial details on half the heavy hitters in Palm Beach. Look at this one, Jack Morganthau. I know Jack. Wow! He's got a lot of stuff overseas that I'll bet the IRS or his ex-wife would love to know about. An oil company in Libya? I don't think U.S. companies are allowed to do business there. This could be damaging information in the wrong hands. It looks like someone got into the computer at Fairfield & Ellis and struck it rich. What are they planning to use it for, blackmail?"

"I don't know. It was in your insurance friend's top desk drawer. He, or someone he works with, must have access to that computer. Maybe they were prospecting for the names of wealthy people to sell their deal to and got more than they bargained for."

Frank scratched his chin. I could see the wheels turning. "We need to drive to the end of the street, wrap these papers around a brick and pretend we never saw them."

He put his big hand on my shoulder and gave me that look my father gave when he was explaining that I shouldn't get into fights but was pleased that a bully had gotten what was coming to him.

"All I wanted to know was: Do bad people own my policy? You come back with personal financial information on some very powerful players. If anyone knows we've got this stuff they'll be a dozen more people wanting us both dead. It's like I send you for a loaf of bread and you steal the bakery."

I started the car. "Tim Ryan must have a friend at the investment firm who got him these printouts."

"Tony, you wore gloves?"

"Of course."

"No one saw you, for sure?"

I didn't see anyone. Possibly someone caught me diving out the window or just saw the car leaving."

"Unless you plan to throw this stuff in the lake, which I know you won't do, get rid of the car, just in case."

"Frankie, this guy Ryan is a hustler. He has to know this list could be exploited for serious money. Let's hope he didn't start the process."

"Any dates on this stuff?"

"I didn't see any, but I haven't had time to go through all the pages yet."

I knew his answer but felt I should ask. "I'm supposed to meet with Sonja. Should I tell her anything?"

"No way! She works for the police. You'll compromise her."

He gave me that look, as though he were about to dispense his pearls of wisdom about women.

"This meeting business or pleasure, Tony?"

"I sure wish it were pleasure, but her husband's a great guy. Course, the fact she's not the least bit interested in me makes it a little easier to be a gentleman."

Frank smiled, "That's getting to be my problem with all women."

I was going to suggest Barbara, but decided to mind my own business.

"All the parts still working, Frank?"

He opened the door, stepped out, and then stuck his head back in the window. "You know all those 'youth is wasted on the young' clichés? They're true. Back when we were young and dating twenty-year-olds with great bodies, we had no time for foreplay. When you get old and foreplay is necessary for both of us, our bodies aren't quite as foreplayable."

He laughed at himself, as he likes to do. "Is that a real word, Tony? foreplayable? I like it."

"Goodbye, Frank."

I put the roof down, stuffed the papers into the brief case in the trunk, and headed back to my hotel room.

It was 10:15. I was meeting Sonja for lunch. That would give me some time to look over the papers and decide what to do.

# Chapter 9

I locked the door to my room and spread the papers out on the bed. It wasn't all juicy stuff. A lot included details on assets, such as ownership, values, and, in some cases, beneficiaries or contingent owners in the event of a death. There were even a few notes on who got along with whom in a particular family. This firm clearly handled an entire family's wealth, and probably made all their major decisions — very private stuff, some of it quite damaging if it got out. I wondered, was Ryan using this information to learn enough about people to sell his policies, or was he threatening to reveal things if they didn't buy?

No, I thought. He's making a large commission on the original purchase, and a second commission when the policy is sold. There had to be people in these pages with the power to have him silenced. He had to be smart enough to not push it.

As I matched the personal letters to the asset sheets I realized that Ryan must have had this information for some time. The pages had been worked over, lost their crispness. George Somersby had gotten a letter two years ago in November. It was now early April. His letter mentioned his collection of rare prints. Ryan was being safe. He stayed away from the Libyan oil deals and tended to mention things that could be public knowledge. I felt a little more comfortable knowing he'd had the papers for over two years and no one had blown him up yet. I guessed that meant the list was still a secret.

The phone rang. I couldn't reach it without crawling over papers, so I scooted off the end of the bed and picked up the phone.

"Hello, baby, we still on for lunch?" Sonja's voice was a purr, a slight Spanish accent, probably gained from her Argentina-born mother.

"Sure, where's good for you"

"How about Bice? We can sit outside in the alley. Can we make it 12:30?"

"No problem. See you there."

I hung up and sat for a moment. She could definitely help. What to tell and not tell?

As I started to pick up the papers to lock them in the closet safe, I noticed a few pages scattered on the floor. One had turned over; there was writing on the back. A name scribbled then crossed out and erased.

The phone number was clear. Then what looked like V-7, which didn't sound like a room number.

I didn't want to be late for Sonja so I hurried to get dressed and organized. I called the valet for my car, and then stood for a minute holding the phone. Why not? I dialed the number.

"Hello, Boca Raton Resort, may I help you?"

I was a little taken back by the Boca. "Do you have a room V-7?"

"Yes sir, those are the private villas on the golf course. May I ring that villa?"

"No. Thank you, no." I put down the phone. What would I

say? Hi, are you with the mob? Do you know Tim Ryan? Are you planning to kill Frank?

I needed a plan and had no idea what it would be.

Better meet Sonja.

# Chapter 10

B ice Ristorante in Palm Beach is known for its slow-cooked "nonna style" sauce.

I like to sit outside. A half dozen tables line the brick and marble sidewalk in a secluded alleyway between Peruvian and Worth avenues. Marble table tops with iron bases, linen napkins, and a bouquet of wildflowers on each table creates an exceptional ambience. It reminds me of its sister restaurant, Bice Milan.

As I looked for Sonja, I realized that, for the nearly twenty years I've known her, she has never been late. She would consider it disrespectful. Her mother raised five daughters on her own in the tough Riviera Beach area, just north of here. The mother knew what a double-edged sword good looks can be, and raised her girls like ugly ducklings. There were no mirrors in the house. Manners, respect, good grades were all that mattered, and a quick slap met anyone who didn't get it.

The result was dramatic. Sonja has high cheek bones, full lips, almond shaped eyes, straight jet-black hair, and a body that won't quit. After I got to know her, I remember marveling at how her looks could attract attention she barely seemed to notice.

She was waving from a table next to the Chanel window. Not her style.

Sonja stood with her tanned arms outstretched. We hugged. Before I could push in her chair, she said, "Notice the street clothes."

I had. In fact, every guy in the place probably noticed what she calls street clothes. The loose-fitting tan blouse and baggy slacks couldn't hide that body. She'd get attention in a sack.

"Sergeant Perez. About time they got smart and promoted you. Save money on all that fancy lab equipment, just use a woman's intuition."

"Thanks, Tony. How did you know I got the job?"

"It was in the 'Shiny Sheet'. I subscribe by mail to make sure you and Frank are staying out of trouble. I love it. Every week, same stuff different people. Guys dressing up as Florida power inspectors, one checks the power, the other checks out with the jewelry. I look on the society page, and a woman is divorcing her husband for the third time. She's giving him half a million a year in alimony so he can live comfortably until she needs him again. What a town!"

Sonja was laughing. "Let's order, Tony. We're keeping this nice young man waiting."

"Non ce una problema, Senora," the waiter replied with a heavy Italian accent.

"Come si chiama?" I asked the waiter.

"Giovanni Ipiacene," he replied

Sonja, still smiling from my story, passed the large one page menu to the waiter. "The ravioli with porcini mushrooms, and can I have extra red sauce on the side? It's so good." She continued, "My friend, whose father was born in Milano, will have the veal scaloppini with black olives, capers, and extra artichokes."

She put her hand on my forearm. "Did I get that right, Tony?"

Giavanni, not used to having a woman in charge, looked to see if I was offended.

Seeing I was OK, he said, "Milano is a beautiful city. I am from Tortona, which is south of Geneva. You have been to Italy?"

"Yes, I have been to Milan many times. I stay at the Gray, near La Scala. I have driven through Tortona to Geneva."

I winked. "Lot of Mafia in Geneva. They control the ports."

"I would not know about these things. You like a nice Chianti?"

I nodded. "Si, grazie, una botiglia foso vechia."

Giavanni smiled his approval and left the table.

Sonja said, "What did you order?"

"I asked for a seasoned, classic Italian red. You'll love it."

"OK, Tony. What's with the Mafia bit?"

"Oh, nothing."

"Tony, I can read you like a book. You didn't bring that up for the fun of it. It was to get a rise out of me. What do you want to know?"

"How come you're only a sergeant? Reading minds ought to be worth at least a captain."

I tried to distract her. "You said Alex had a problem. How can I help?"

She smiled and pointed a finger at my chest. "I know what you're doing, Tony. It won't work. I haven't forgotten the Mafia remark. His company is owned by an outfit in Boston called Proteus. Do you know anyone there?"

"I don't know the company, but someone I know might. I'll check." Sonja looked me straight in the eye. This time she didn't smile. "What's with the Mafia remark?"

I knew she had the respect of other law enforcement agencies based on more than her looks. I had hoped to get her help without revealing too much.

"I know a few of the 'good fellas' from Boston who vacation in

Boca," I said. "Are any doing business down here?"

"Years ago Boca was put on some people's map by Lefty Rosenthal, remember him? The main character in the movie *Casino*. I'd say that rates a yes."

I decided to tell her the story. We'd done this before. If I started to tell her something that would compromise her position as a police officer she would shake her head and I'd stop. So I talked in general terms about some computer sheets I had found that listed a lot of prominent people in Palm Beach, maybe people Tim Ryan had insured. I finished with my phone call to the mysterious number that turned out to be Villa 7.

Sonja listened quietly. When I finished, she said, "Be careful. There are some jams I can't get you out of."

She picked up her cell and walked out onto the sidewalk. Neither of us think it polite to use a cell phone in a restaurant. I also suspected she didn't want anyone to overhear her call, including me.

Giovanni arrived with the food.

"You have been to the Bice in Milano?"

"Yes, I have a friend who loves the opera. We go to a performance a La Scala, and oftentimes we go to Bice afterward."

He pulled out the chair for Sonja. "Buon appettito," and was gone.

She took a bite of her ravioli and poured on the extra sauce. "Villa 7 is rented for the season by a waste disposal company owned by a Vitorio Pagano from Chicago. My contact doesn't think anyone is staying there now. He's getting me more information and will call back."

"Pagano? What do you know about him?"

"Let's wait until we get more details." Sonja was frowning. Not a good sign, I thought, but typical Sonja. Get the facts straight before offering any information.

"Okay, Tony, explain to me what this guy Ryan does."

"The background to what he does is this: Investment groups started buying life insurance policies from people who were sick and needed the money before they died."

She nodded. "A person has a million dollar policy. They get a quarter or a half million, while they're alive, to pay medical bills. The buyers hold the policy and receive a handy return when they die."

"Right! Then these investment groups realized that competition has created a market where certain types of life policies are under-priced. They began buying policies that people didn't want, and holding them until death. The obvious next step was for them to create their own inventory. This is where Ryan comes in. He lends money to people to buy a policy on their life, which he will later sell on the open market for a profit."

Sonja was smiling, "So Ryan gets an easy sale, then makes money again when the policy is sold. But what's in it for the guy who gets insured?"

"He gets free coverage for a couple of years, and then splits the profit when it's sold."

Sonja shrugged, "Sounds like everybody wins. What's the prob-?"

She stopped in the middle of her sentence and stared at me. "Pagano is buying the policies!"

I realized she knew more about Pagano than she had let on.

She nodded and said, "I see. So, instead of selling to a legitimate insurance company, Ryan sells the policy to a company owned by the boys from Boca who know how to increase returns with some early claims?"

"Exactly! I need to know if they are the group that bought Frank's policy."

Sonja looked away for a long thirty seconds, her analytical mind processing the steps. "But why would a policy on a healthy person give a good return? That means the insurance company that sold it made a bad deal. "

She never missed a trick.

I shook my head. "Not really. Stock companies sell policies knowing most will get dropped or replaced by someone looking for a new sales commission. So they lowball the price to increase sales. More sales make their stock go up. High charges on policies that are dropped are profitable. They sell you a policy and hope you don't keep it."

She glanced at her watch. "Darn! I've got a 2:30 meeting. We need to talk more. I'll call you again as soon as I hear from my man."

We walked outside. I handed the valet our tickets.

The two o'clock sun had caused beads of sweat to form on the foreheads and upper lips of the small group waiting at the curbside valet. Sonja's Latin skin seemed to relish the afternoon heat. I watched as she checked the messages on her cell, gesturing toward me with each, a nod or a shrug, then quickly cancelling or saving to listen later. Finally she raised her index finger and smiled. This was the one she'd been waiting for. I stood close, taking pleasure in the envious looks of both men and women who probably thought we were a couple.

This time her look was intense, the smile gone. "Vitorio Pagano!"

I shrugged. "Ya?"

She continued, repeating word for word the message on her cell as though it had been read off a police teletype. "Older gentleman; mid-seventies; dapper dresser; very smooth; born into the Italian Mafia; controlled Chicago and the Midwest for several decades; no jail time; lives in Boca in the winter."

Two valets pulled up to the curb, a 2006 deep blue Bentley convertible and a used Chevy Impala. Sonja stepped toward the Chevy. The valet was holding the door and smiling. I guessed what was on the kid's mind. Sonja should be driving the Bentley.

"Tony," she said, "Go to the West Palm library, over at the end of Clematis. Look up old Boca and Chicago newspapers. Maybe check the Internet. Find what you can on Vitorio Pagano."

I nodded, still relishing the stares of those who thought we were a couple.

Her look was serious. "You said you'd seen the movie *Casino?*" Without waiting for an answer, she continued. Her tone was flat and business like, "Lefty Rosenthal, look for him too. It may give you some extra background. You need to understand who you may be dealing with. These are not Boy Scouts."

She tipped the valet holding the car door and stepped in.

Detective Sergeant Sonja Perez, a member of Palm Beach's finest, drove off in her unmarked Chevy.

I took a deep breath. If these "gentlemen" in Boca owned the company that bought Frank's policy, you had to wonder, what were the odds they were going to wait for him to die of old age?

I needed to find them before they came looking for Frank.

# Chapter 11

Feeling a little sleepy from the Chianti and scaloppini, I decided to take advantage of the warm, nearly cloudless day with a walk to clear my head. When the second valet arrived, I gave him ten and asked if he'd hold the car a little longer.

I headed back through the alleyway of outdoor tables where we'd just, as they say, "done lunch" and continued along the wide marble walk that runs through to Worth Avenue. No space here is wasted. My journey took me past brightly lit windows with clothing by Domenico Vacca, Francesca Romana, and Borrelli. You'd think you were in Italy but for the two "Eye of the Needle" shops featuring ladieswear in Nantucket pinks.

Worth Avenue is a most appropriate name. High Net Worth would be even more fitting. At one end is Neiman Marcus, where you can purchase a very nice necktie or a walnut-sized jar of eye-wrinkle cream for under $250. Just under. At the other end is the Everglades Club, which you could easily join if you could pick your great-grandparents. Dozens of top end clothing, jewelry, art, and antique stores lie between.

On the corner of a building across from my Italian Alley, I spotted a shin-level faucet with a sign, "Doggie Bar." My fantasy of dogs sitting at a bar discussing what foolish tricks their masters and mistresses had performed that day was interrupted. Out of the corner of my eye, a well-proportioned brunette with an athletic stride appeared in front of the Ralph Lauren store. As I stood admiring her slim waist and toned arms, she stepped inside, came back out, glanced across in my direction, and began to slowly pace up and down. Finally, she stopped in front of the store, and, while running her fingers through her hair, glanced in my direction.

I watched the breeze dance along the fringe of her ruffled skirt, lifting it to reveal a few inches of thigh, then releasing it to slide back before the next wind pushed it again, always to a different spot. I'd recognize those legs anywhere. It was her, my mirror friend from the Palm Beach Grill.

Suddenly, she turned and went inside, as though she'd been called.

I sprinted across the narrow street. Hesitating at the door like a kid on his first day of school, I leaned toward the side window and was peering between the mannequins, when I realized an impeccably dressed older gentleman was holding the door and motioning for me to come inside. He had swept-back white hair and was wearing an off-white linen jacket and a purple tie.

He greeted me as though I were an old friend visiting. "I just had the most delightful Dover sole at Taboo. I love it pan fried. They get it fresh. It often sells out before I arrive. I take a late lunch; noontimes are busy here." He held out his hand. "My name is André. May I help you find something?"

No wonder he's so well dressed, I thought. He's a living advertisement for Ralph Lauren.

Feeling more than a little awkward, I stammered, "No, I'm just looking." André must have thought, "You sure are!"

I was trying to be polite, but my eyes were darting about the room. Realizing she had to be on the second level, I gave André

a forced grin, half sprinted past the rows of men's suits and acces-
sories, and started up the stairs, head down. As I reached the top
step, I raised my eyes. There she was, her hand on the arm of a tall
man facing the tie counter. She looked over and smiled, as though
she'd been expecting me. Flummoxed, I turned to the right, trying
to look as though I knew where I was going. She seemed to know
I had followed her into the store, and was enjoying my discomfort.
Her eyes tracked me as I tried on a jacket that was four sizes too big
in the waist and many too short in the arms.

I was starting to feel very foolish. Maybe that look she had given
me the night before wasn't a come-on. Maybe it wasn't her finger
tips I had felt slide across my back, not her voice that whispered
good night. Maybe she had no idea who I was.

No. She was looking directly at me, her hand at her mouth,
stifling a laugh. I started toward her, my mind racing for something to say. No need. Her tall friend turned from the counter and
quickly escorted her down the stairs. From the top of the stairs
I watched. She turned at the door, gave me a two-fingered wave
and smiled. I waited a minute to seem less obvious, and then
headed down the steps. André, who had been watching the whole
encounter, leaned toward me. "Taboo for lunch, you'll enjoy it
there at the bar."

He'd seen my obvious game; was he telling me something? Had
he seen her there? I forced a smiled and left.

As I started back across Worth, a horn began beeping. It was
Frank in his Jaguar. He must have seen me follow the mystery
woman into Ralph Lauren, and waited.

He pulled over, and pushed open the passenger-side door.

"Tony, never mind the million-dollar ass. We need to talk."

I hesitated, but got in.

"I've been looking for you. Sonja called my cell as soon as she left Bice. She's worried. What did you tell her?"

"Only the basics, that I had found a computer list with names of people Ryan may have insured. I think she can help us."

"Well, Sonja's concerned. She told me about Pagano. If some of the names on the computer list are people Ryan insured, they might also be people someone plans to kill. And that someone is going to come looking for that list."

He started to drive off.

"Hey, Frank, where are we going?"

"Have I ever given you bad advice?"

I pretended to think a minute, but the answer was obvious.

"No, can't say you have."

"That brunette you've got 'the hots' for, could be very hazardous to your health."

"I know, but what a way to die."

"That's not what I'm talking about, Tony. She's a cognoscenti."

"You mean a connoisseur? She's Italian?"

"Giacometti, as in Alberto, the sculptor. That's his granddaughter, Gabriella. She's got a Ph.D. in everything Italian. Art, music, fashion, you name it. Being his favorite granddaughter got her style and class, but others grabbed the money. The word is she makes a very nice living as a personal shopper and art collector for some of your boys in Boca, maybe for Vitorio himself."

I leaned back in the seat. "At least you can say I've got good taste."

We had circled the block and were back in front of Bice.

"I should drive you to the airport and send you home to Bean Town, but I know how stubborn you are. You'd be back tomorrow. Besides, I need you."

I looked at Frank and grinned. "She could tell me a lot of things I'd like to know."

He looked directly at me and put his hand on my shoulder. "Maybe she could, and maybe curiosity didn't kill the cat."

He hesitated a few seconds, and then continued, "Look Tony, I got you down here because I was worried about me. Now I'm worried about us. That's not progress. Be very careful of this Gabriella. People don't work for Pagano unless they are very loyal. Let's not get us both killed." He wasn't smiling.

He drove off, and I drove off. Frank probably knew where he was going. That made one of us.

# Chapter 12

I drove on, but my mind had switched to automatic pilot, alternating between images of Gabriella's smiling two-fingered wave and Frank's clear look of concern. Should I head back to Worth Avenue, see if she was still hitting the stores? What would I say? Hey, didn't we exchange looks at the Palm Beach Grill? Oh, by the way, I hear you work for that Chicago mobster, Vitorio Pagano. I'd like to ask you some questions about him. Or maybe, you've got a great ass, how about drinks at my place?

As I was sorting out my thoughts, the car had taken a right on South County, then another right.I was headed for the front door of Taboo.

Frank's words came back, "Maybe curiosity didn't kill the cat." I stepped on the gas and headed for the bridge that I had crossed nearly eight hours earlier on my way to visit Mr. Ryan. Frank was right. If they owned his policy, there was no rush. They could kill him today or five years from now. The person with the list was a threat today. I had to learn all I could about these guys, and quick.

The library, at the foot of Clematis Street, toward the Lake, faces a large open square with a fountain in the center. Kids were splashing in the fountain. Couples young and old sat talking or reading on the benches shaded by the banyan trees on the edges of the square. An elderly woman, as gray and worn as the sweater draped over her shoulders, looked up and pointed to the sky. "Beautiful day, isn't it?"

She had a kindness in her eyes, and the clarity of her diction made me wonder what turn of chance or birth placed her alone on this bench, instead of the courtyard of the Breakers or Brazilian Court enjoying afternoon tea with friends.

I smiled. "Yes it is."

No time to chat, it was 3:15, and the library closed at 4:00. I hurried up the steps and headed for the information desk.

The woman behind the desk was absorbed in something on a computer screen. I stood quietly for a minute with no response. I gently cleared my throat.

A blandly attractive woman, with no makeup and slightly graying hair in a bun turned in her chair to face me. She smiled and asked in an official but very pleasant voice, "I'm Grace May. How may I help you?"

"I'd like a book on Giacometti, the sculptor."

I don't know where that came from. I was supposed to be looking for newspaper articles on Lefty Rosenthal the gambler and Vitorio Pagano the mobster.

Her face lit up. "Yes, one of my favorites." She led me down a long row of shelves that opened into an alcove with a small table and several comfortable-looking chairs.

"This area is our art section. We have several very fine books on Giacometti."

She struggled with a slightly oversized book and placed it on the table. *Alberto Giacometti the Complete Graphics*. "This one has wonderful representations of his works."

She flipped through the pages, stopping at a very dark painting of his mother. "He painted this before the war, when he was still in Paris. Interesting."

I nodded. "Yes, but I guess I think of him as a sculptor. Those thin abstract statues. Do you have something more biographical, more about his family, his personal life? It helps one understand what made him create. Don't you think?"

"Yes, here's a book that does just that. It's written by the French poet Yves Bonnefoy. A poet writing on a sculptor seems quite fitting to me."

I liked how Grace May's mind worked. I took the book and flipped through the pages. "Yes, this is perfect."

"We close in a few minutes. Are you able to come back tomorrow? We open at nine-thirty."

I held the book close. "This is just what I was looking for. Could I take it and read it tonight?" I could have added, "To help make conversation with his granddaughter."

When I was younger, the library was where you told your mother you were going on a school night, when you were really hanging out with friends. I now realized a friend at the library could be a real asset. I gave Grace May my best smile, still holding the book against my chest.

"How did you end up in this line of work?" I asked.

She surprised me. I was expecting, "I love to read."

"When my husband died, I had three young boys and no money. This job was available. I'm an artist and sculptor, which is why I've always loved Giacometti's surrealism."

As she continued on, I nodded and smiled, only half understanding what she was talking about, and thinking I needed to buy a dictionary.

At the front desk, I stopped and took out my wallet.

"I don't have a library card. Here's my license and one hundred dollars. Will you trust me with this beautiful book?"

She pushed my hand away. "Yes, but it will be our secret. You will bring it back in the morning? I don't want to get fired."

As we reached the door, I asked. "Grace, do you have local newspapers on microfilm so I might look up some history? I'm thinking of moving to this area, probably somewhere between Palm Beach and Boca. I'd like to get some background."

"Yes, of course, come early. Nine o'clock. I'll let you in. Monday morning is busy. In case you hadn't noticed, there are a lot of retired people down here. They seem to finish their books on the weekends. Funny isn't it? They have the whole week now, but after years of working, the habit of reading mainly on the weekends can't be broken."

She held out her hand. "Good day, Mr…?"

"Tauck, Anthony Tauck."

She wasn't what she'd seemed at first. People usually aren't, but the reminder of my high school librarian brought back the Anthony, as in "Anthony! No talking in the library."

# Chapter 13

Back at the Brazilian, I threw on a jacket and fresh shirt, picked up my book, and headed downstairs to Café Boulud. The indoor restaurant is located beyond the bar where I'd had coffee that morning before visiting Tim Ryan. The room was small and tastefully decorated with bright abstract paintings and photos of the rich and famous. The courtyard in the center of the hotel was again full of formally dressed contributors.

The maitre'd smiled and shook my hand. "Good evening, sir."

I pointed to a small table in the corner. I didn't want to be disturbed and sitting with my back to the wall is an old habit. I took the waiter's advice and ordered the Coq au Vin, a French version of my mother's chicken cacciatore, and the house burgundy.

I sipped my wine, skimmed the book, and savored one of the best Coq Au Vins I'd ever had. The hint of cognac, garlic and burgundy in the sauce enhanced the chicken breast and added just the right touch to the sautéed mushrooms, carrots and pearl onions. Flipping back and forth to different sections of the book, I gradually chose the areas that I thought might engage Gabriella's interest, if we chanced to meet.

Alberto Giacometti, born in Italian-speaking Switzerland in 1901, died in 1966. That would make his favorite granddaughter close to fifty. She didn't look it.

He had been a friend of the existentialist Jean-Paul Sartre, I'll keep away from that subject. I can barely pronounce existentialism, let alone explain what it is. She'd bury me.

When Giacometti was in his early twenties, he had a companion die suddenly. He became fixated on the transitory nature of life, living mainly in hotels and cafés as though he was just passing through. Definitely a conversation piece.

His early work, both drawings and sculpture, was miniature. Much as he tried, he couldn't seem to sculpt anything lifesize. Another point to discuss, probably good for several drinks.

I closed the book, put my hands behind my head, and leaned back in my chair.

Where was I going with this? The woman seemed, at best, an indirect route to Frank's problem, but she was the only connection I knew of. She had seemed approachable on a male-female level. Would she freeze up if Vitorio were mentioned? Would bringing him up connect me to the list? Both times I'd seen her, something invited me back. The sexual attraction was obvious, but I knew there was more, and Frank's warnings that she was super-intelligent only acted as gasoline on a fire.

# Chapter 14

She must have been watching for me. As I reached the top step the door opened and Grace May greeted me with, "Good morning, Anthony. Did you enjoy the book?"

"I loved it. You were so nice to trust me. I was fascinated by Giacometti's early stage with miniatures. Was that something psychological?"

She had put on a little lipstick and let her hair down. The look was now artist-hippy, not librarian-bookworm. Her dress revealed a little more skin, and a cute figure. I wondered if the change was for me.

Before she could get into a dissertation on Giacometti's psyche, I steered her toward the computer.

"Is there a Boca newspaper?"

"Yes, the *Boca Raton News*, for a different project?"

"Can we find articles on Frank 'Lefty' Rosenthal?"

"The movie *Casino*, sure." She pulled up a screen, FrankRosenthal. com.

I read his bio. Probably the best sports handicapper of all time. Still consults for several sports betting operations. Ran Las Vegas casinos for the Chicago mob. Came to Boca in 1988, after losing his license in Vegas, etc.

"He's a sports handicapper, not a hit man," I thought. "He can't be my guy." But the Chicago connection was interesting.

Grace gave me a puzzled look. "Why are you interested in him?"

"Just curious. I saw the movie, and recently I read an article about the Mob vacationing in Boca. I grew up in an Italian section of Boston where the Mafia was present. It's just a side interest."

She smiled a knowing smile. "It is a fascinating phenomenon. I've seen *The Godfather* films more times than I can count."

She seemed to buy my story, so I decided to push further. "How would I look up articles on other personalities? Say Vitorio Pagano of Chicago."

"That's easy. We have a tie-in with other libraries on the Internet. Come to my desk." She quickly had the *Chicago Tribune* on the screen. "How do you spell the name?"

Sure enough, a photo of an older man standing with friends in front of a restaurant appeared on the screen. He was graying but appeared very fit. A head shot showed an exceptionally handsome man. He had contributed some paintings to the Chicago Art Institute. The trustees were questioning whether they should take them, considering whom he was alleged to be.

The noise of a door banging shut intruded on our search.

The large clock above the door said 9:45. The weekend readers were streaming in as predicted.

I took her hand, "Thanks, Grace, you've been great. I'll be back for more Giacometti. I just wanted to bring your book back before you got fired."

"Anytime I can help, Anthony." She gave me a smile that was not librarian.

I started my car and sat checking my cell. Three messages. I didn't listen, just pressed the redial.

"Sonja, what's up, any news?"

"Hi Tony. No, but that's not why I called. I was wondering if you had seen Mrs. 'Body by' Fisher?"

I had asked Sonja for help when I was working on Mrs. Fisher's case. We had kidded about what a great figure she had for a seventy-year-old woman.

"Yes, I see her almost every time I come down. Why?"

"I heard Ms. Giacometti has done some appraisals for her, some Italian Renaissance stuff."

Sonya paused. She was waiting for my reaction.

Frank must have told her about my interest in Gabriella. It seemed she was encouraging what Frank discouraged. Typical Sonja, always hoping I'd settle down with a "nice girl."

I wasn't sure I wanted more advice, so I waited.

"You still there, Tony?"

"Ya."

"Be careful."

# Chapter 15

Harold has been Mrs. Fisher's butler for as long as I've known her. He's a Miami Heat fan and loves to kid me about the sometimes lackluster Celtics. As we stepped out onto the back patio, I was trying to turn the discussion onto the Patriots again being in a Super Bowl.

Mrs. Fisher was seated under an umbrella at the far end of the patio toward the lake. She had been diminutive woman when we first met, and the last twenty of her ninety years had shrunk her even more. But her voice was as loud and clear as an actress projecting to the back row. She had that Ruth Gordon spunk.

I had been trying to convince myself that my interest in Gabriella was all business, rationalizing that she was a potential gateway to people who might be a threat to Frank, and I should find out as much as I could about her. Mrs. Fisher's interest in Italian art might move me a step closer.

From the patio I could look across the lake to West Palm. The sun was low. I had to squint to see Mrs. Fisher seated at a table adorned with fruits, teacups and a large silver vase filled with flowers I was sure had come from her own garden.

I bent to take her hand and gave her a kiss on the cheek.

"It's so nice to see you looking well, Mrs. Fisher."

She held my hand in a firm grip for an extra few seconds. "What mystery are you here to solve, Anthony?"

Then she laughed and only half kidding said, "I'm sure you can't tell, professional secrecy or some such thing. And after all these years, can't I get you to call me Harriet? 'Mrs. Fisher' sounds so old."

Harold poured my tea and offered me a petit-four which I waved away.

"Your family is well, Mrs.-I mean-Harriet?" I've always had trouble calling women of her age by first names. Each time I do, I imagine a look or a cuff from my mother.

"Yes, Anthony, we have all gotten over that episode. In some ways it was a good thing. Those involved were on my late-husband Harry's side. They'd been spoiled rotten by their mother, and expected when Harry died they'd cash in. Unfortunately for them Bill Bingham structured Harry's trusts to provide for me until death. They are still waiting but, thanks to you and a few others, much more patiently. That is all past. My life has been too blessed to hold a grudge."

"Bill Bingham, as in Bingham, DuPont?"

"Why, yes, they handled all Harry's affairs, and now mine. They pay my bills, taxes, credit cards, and even my staff."

I thought I'd push it. "They have an investment group, Fairfield & Ellis, that manages their client's assets."

"Yes, Harry had investments all over the world. They handled them all. Some sort of tax offsetting, Harry called it."

She paused, and then continued. "I was married to a fine, caring man. He's been gone twenty-five years this month. I still think of him every day."

She reached out a thin arm and put her empty cup on the silver tray.

"Fitzgerald said, 'The rich are different,' and they are, but not in the important ways. We all feel love and loss. I miss my husband with the same feelings as any other woman who has been with a good man."

"I guess if you have more money than you'll ever need, it doesn't enter into life's equation." I realized, as I said it, that Harriet was one of the few people that I could say that to without offending her.

"That's right," she said. "I learned to be a good cook, even though we always had help. I became a fine sailor, although we had a crew for the boat. I pursue my interests. I was just never attracted to numbers."

I knew she had published books on cooking and gardening that were considered unique, but I needed to change the subject.

"And, as I recall you became somewhat of an expert on art."

"Yes, I'm just looking at some new acquisitions." She rose from her chair more quickly than her years should have allowed. "Come see."

Her library was not covered in the dark paneling you might expect, but in light golden oak, as though it had actually been used as a library and not the room gentlemen retired to for a smoke after dinner.

"This is a Boccioni, an early twentieth-century Italian sculptor and painter. You like-a?" She used her hands as though she were Boccioni describing his own work.

"Yes, I like-a," I replied, "but don't understand-a."

She laughed, "It's called the 'Street Enters the House'. Boccioni was a Futurist."

As I stared at the abstract painting of a woman leaning forward, away from the artist, toward buildings and boat masts, I tried to think of a half-intelligent comment. Finally, seeing the houses bend toward the street, I said, "Now I see where Frank Gehry, the architect, got his ideas."

"That's a very interesting comment, Anthony. These were shown to me by an intriguing young woman. You know of Giacometti?"

"The sculptor? Of course; I love his tall, skinny pieces."

"This young woman is his granddaughter, Gabriella. Fascinating woman and very articulate, speaks six languages and knows her way around the art world. At my ancient age I'm hard to impress, but I may buy this painting simply on her recommendation."

"I like it, but it looks more like a woman entering a town." I tried to seem more interested in the painting than in Gabriella, but Harriet's pause allowed me the opening. "How did you meet this Gabriella?"

"I was seated next to her at a dinner party. She was with young George Bingham. He followed his father into the firm. George seemed quite taken by her, but I believe he's too much like his mother, dull, no playfulness, takes himself too seriously. He's trying to be his father, but he's got his mother's brain, poor thing."

She stopped and pointed her finger at my chest. "She should be with you."

I held up my palms in protest, said nothing, and waited.

"I know something about you, Anthony. Word gets around, even in my circle of friends. I never told you this, but I did a little detective work after you helped with my problem. You were married once into a nice Palm Beach family. I know your former mother-in-law quite well. She spoke very highly of you, said you were a bright and principled young man."

I rolled my eyes but said nothing. I had only seen the witch once in the fifteen years since my divorce from her daughter. She gave me a nod and a frosty smile. She hadn't come from anything special, but once her kind gets in, they try to keep everyone else out. I always thought she resented what I'd had with Elizabeth. Unlike her, my marriage was for love. I never cared to be "in."

"I'm going to introduce you to this Giacometti woman. She'll give you a real run for your money." She chuckled to herself, and then nodded to the butler standing in the doorway. "Harold will see you to the door."

# Chapter 16

Turning out of the Fisher driveway onto Coconut Way, heading south toward the hotel, I picked up my cell, called Sonja, and got her service. Not wanting to leave anything specific I thought for a minute.

Gabriella was in some way associated with Vitorio Pagano. She also dated George Bingham, whose law firm owned Fairfield & Ellis. Tim Ryan had Fairfield & Ellis's client list, or used to.

How were they connected?

As I turned onto Peruvian, I left a message "Sonja, what do you know about George Bingham? He dates our friend."

I had barely reached my room when she called back.

"Tony, I told you Alex needed your help? He's the guy, Bingham. Can you meet me at Taboo at 6:30?"

Putting down the phone, I let my body fall back across the bed, rubbed my temples, and tried to make sense of all this.

Tim Ryan somehow gained access to the list of wealthy families.

He would send them a letter in which, to get their interest, he inferred he had information on their finances. He'd go see them, and offer free life insurance coverage with a profit at the end.

Did Gabriella manipulate George to get the list for Pagano, who then gave it to Ryan, who sold the insurance, then resold polices back to Pagano, who planned to kill them for the insurance?

Most potential clients would have called their advisors to check out Ryan and his scheme before they took action. Maybe that's where George Bingham came in? The firm gave him the job of checking out Ryan's program.

But how did Bingham meet Gabriella Giacometti? No way it was a coincidence.

Now I was meeting Sonja about Bingham, who was causing problems for her husband Alex. Bingham was showing up in too many places.

I rolled onto my side to check the time; 6:10, just time for a quick shower.

# Chapter 17

Coming in from the still bright sunlight, it took six or eight steps into the narrow lounge area before my eyes adjusted to the dim light. There was Sonja, early as always, waving from the far end of the bar.

The early dinner crowd tends to be upscale and middle aged. This night mainly women, dressed to dine in their best jewelry, sat and talked in groups of twos and threes. Sonya had found two empty seats toward the end of the bar. Beyond us two men stood drinking martinis and trying to impress two younger women, who in turn were trying to impress them.

Sonya turned her stool to face me, "As they say in your business, the plot thickens."

"No kidding. The broth Frank asked me to taste is now a thick stew, and a little bigger bowl than I ordered."

I took a sip of the Dewar's that she had waiting. "I've been trying to connect Gabriella and George. What do you think?"

She was shaking her head. With her index finger to her lips, and her eyes looking down, she again shook her head. "Tony, I know that you're thinking — that she's playing him. Maybe she is, but you need to listen to this."

She looked up, and half smiled. "I was told, very hush, hush

George has a three-year-old daughter and a mistress living in Lauderdale. She wasn't suitable to marry a Bingham so the family moved her out of town and gives her money."

"So he's not my competition for Gabriella."

"Tony, you're every woman's type, tall, dark, handsome, and sensitive. I don't know him, but odds are you're safe. "

"If you think that, maybe I'm your type."

She gave me a wink. "Right after Frank."

"You asked me about Proteus?"

"Yes," she said. "Alex is the financial guy for his company. George's law firm is their corporate counsel. He's doing a lot of underhanded stuff to make Alex look bad. He's trying to force him out, get his friend the job."

"You remember my ex-partner Phil?"

She nodded, "He came down to play golf with you last fall. Nice guy.

I continued, "He has Proteus as a group-benefits client; plays golf with the president. He remembers you. He'll fix it." She put her long slim fingers with the bright red nails on my forearm and gave it a squeeze. "Appreciate your help, Tony. "Alex says, 'What George Bingham lacks in brains, he makes up for in cunning.' He's not a nice man."

The bartender was jiggling the ice in my empty glass.

"Freshen your drink, sir?" He looked like he'd spent a lot of tips on his perfect smile, to match the blonde hair and broad shoulders, but the artificial light wasn't flattering. His smile lines were crevices in his deeply tanned face. He looked older than his years. I guessed too many late nights followed by days on the beach.

Sonja put her hand over her half-empty glass.

He returned with my Scotch. "I didn't mean to listen in, but were you talking about George Bingham?

"Yes, you know him?"

"Great guy, we grew up together. Always trying to live up to his father's expectations. He'd be better off if he left town, forgot the money.

I remembered André at Ralph Lauren. "Does he come in here?"

"Sure, he stops in a lot."

"Alone?"

"Lately with an attractive Italian woman, an art dealer or something."

He turned away to greet another customer.

Sonja was giggling. "Well, he's got one friend. Could be the source of the list."

I put my arm on Sonja's shoulder like an all-knowing sage. "Here's the deal. Ryan is selling his insurance package. Pagano gets wind of it and wants in. He convinces Ryan to join forces. Tells him he'll get him prospects, puts a dead horse in his bed. Whatever!"

Sonja gave her earthy laugh.

I continued, "It's a perfect fit with Pagano's existing business, creating early deaths. Next Ryan makes contact with George, either using Gabriella, or." I stopped and grabbed her arm. "Hey, find out if George gambles. George has his mother's brain and his father's ambition. Guys with no brains, who want to big-deal it, often gamble."

She was nodding. "Right, he gets in debt and they own him. I might have a source."

She took her cell out of her purse and pointed it at me like a gun. As she swung her bare legs off the chair her skirt rode up above her knees. She pulled it down quickly, looked up to see if the bartender noticed, and headed for the sidewalk, now dark. "Be right back."

I could almost hear her mother telling her. "Cover your legs. Don't give the wrong impression, Sonja."

She was on her way out, punching a number into her phone, when a woman a few stools down stopped her. I had to lean back a little to check her out. She was a very attractive blonde, no surprise for Palm Beach.

After a few minutes Sonja was back.

"Any luck?"

"My friend didn't think so, but he is going to make some inquiries."

"Who's the blonde?"

"She asked about you, thinks you're cute. But you were a football player. Not her type."

"What does that mean?"

Sonja was laughing. "She likes third-basemen. She'd settle for a second-baseman or a shortstop, but you got to be an infielder."

"Really?"

"Twenty years ago she was a hot commodity, partied her way through the American league, but only infielders."

"I could tell her I played shortstop in Little League."

"I don't think she likes little. Besides, after asking about you, she asked the magic question."

"What's that?"

"Is he generous?"

"Sounds like she's moved from infielders to team owners."

"You got it."

"Back to reality, maybe George isn't in on it. All we know is Ryan has a list from George's firm, and Gabriella appears to have a relationship with both George and Pagano."

Sonja was checking her watch. "I've got to get home. We have some friends coming over. You're welcome to stop by."

"No, but thanks, I've got another idea. Go ahead; I'll get the tab. Talk to you tomorrow."

She stood, put her hand on my shoulder, and bent toward me. "People like Pagano have stayed on top as long as they have for a reason. They're cautious. They're patient. They don't buy a policy one day and kill the person the next. I know you are trying to protect Frank, but think about it, you have a list that could bring this whole thing down. You're the one at risk. I don't want to read about you in the *Post's* obituaries."

My first thought was, I need to change cars in the morning.

My second thought was to check the obituaries.

# Chapter 18

Driving back to the Brazilian, I called Frank. We needed to talk, to get together.

"Can't tonight, Tony. I'm going to an art and antique show with a new friend."

I expected the usual quip, but asked anyway, "Anybody interesting?"

"At my age, the art I like is too expensive and the only antiques I get to touch are the women."

I started to tell him my idea. He said he was late, but he'd make the call and see me at Green's in the morning.

On the way to my room, I picked up the *Palm Beach Post* in the lobby. The obituaries listed twenty-two deaths in Palm Beach County, two on the island.

One was young. The other looked like a prospect. James Maguire, eighty-six, died in a car accident. The "survived by's" lived all over the country except for a wife and one daughter still in Palm Beach. He was a member of the Everglades Club and The Bath & Tennis, just the type who would have Bingham oversee his affairs.

Visiting hours were Monday and Tuesday, six to nine p.m.

It was 8:10. No time to cross check with Ryan's list. I needed to pay my respects ASAP. Tollman Funeral Home is across the

Southern Bridge on Washington. The lot was still full. I parked on a side street and walked the block to the home.

People were chatting outside in groups of twos and threes. Not many tears. I guess, at his age, few but the immediate family feel the grief.

I put on my somber look and mounted four steps through the ornate pillars to the double doorway. Inside I surveyed a group of men in the nearly empty room on the right. Recognizing no one, I cautiously entered the large rectangular waiting room. It was crowded with groups of, I guessed, friends and fellow club members. The casket, surrounded by flowers, was at the far end. I decided to join the short line paying respects.

Bingo! Sitting with two women, close to the casket, was a heavy-set man with short dark hair and widow's peak. The same guy I'd seen with his two buddies on Tim Ryan's desk. That must be Tim consoling the family.

The slow line gave me time. When it was my turn, I knelt, said a quick Our Father, and glanced over at the women. Tim was now standing, talking to what looked like a group of Mr. Maguire's peers.

Why not? I stood, waiting for another guest to leave, and then bent down to the seated lady, obviously the widow.

"My condolences, Mrs. Maguire," then I took a chance. The obituary mentioning his being club champion some years ago. I asked, "Had your husband been playing golf recently?"

"Oh, yes, he loved his golf, still played several times a week. Were you a friend from the Club?"

"No, Ma'am. I was only a guest, but was fortunate to have joined his foursome last year. We had a very interesting chat. He gave me a couple of swing tips that were helpful. He was so patient with me."

The daughter, who was listening, started to laugh. "Are you sure you've got the right guy? He taught me to play. Patience was not the word that would apply."

She was slim but shapely with deep blue eyes that seemed to take on an extra glow when she laughed. I couldn't tell if she was putting me on, testing me, or just being herself. I elected the latter.

"I'm sorry. I should have introduced myself. Anthony Tauck. Perhaps your father's mellowed a bit since you were a child."

She laughed again, "Why Mr. Tauck! Are you suggesting my lessons are ancient history?"

Was she was flirting with me? I looked to her mother for help. She was enjoying her daughter's barbs.

"Judging by your mother's age, I'd say your teenage lessons were quite recent."

Her mother, enjoying our connection, took my hand. "Perhaps you and Jennifer should play some time. You could exchange notes on your lessons."

"I'd love nothing better, but Jennifer would be bored to death playing with someone at my level."

"Why don't you call me? I love to beat good-looking men." She reached into her purse and handed me her card.

I noticed others waiting to offer condolences. "I'll get out of the way and let you speak to some of the other guests."

I leaned closer to Jennifer. "When might you be free?"

"Any time after Wednesday, Anthony, maybe Thursday morning?" Her voice was tired.

Nodding, I placed her card in my inside jacket pocket, and turned to go.

"I'll call you to confirm."

Tim was in conversation with several men. I wondered, had they noticed me; were they speculating?

Had I pushed my luck by identifying myself?

I half-jogged to the car, pretty certain that James Maguire was a Ryan client — and that I'd been seen. I climbed in quickly and sat for a second checking the rearview mirror. Then realized I was in Kate's neighborhood. Maybe good to lay low for an hour or two.

I expected her to be surprised to hear my voice. No such luck.

"I know you're in Palm Beach. Why did you wait three days to call me?"

"It's not three days. I got here Saturday night. It's only Monday."

"Doesn't matter, lover boy, come on over."

Katherine was back in Palm Beach where she had lived twenty years ago. Her four kids were young then and her husband was the saxophone player in a popular club called The Bric Yard. They left the area for a gig in Vegas which lasted three years.

Something, which she never completely explained to me, happened that caused them to pack up and leave in the middle of the night. She and her kids settled in Boston, we met, and have been close friends ever since.

She's street smart, a scrapper, a survivor. She had to be to raise four kids on her own with little help from two ex-husbands.

She opened the door and gave me a big hug.

"Hi, honey. That was quick. What did you do? Drive over, then call from the street to test the water before dropping in?"

"I was at Tollman's."

"Anyone I know?"

"Not even anyone I know. Older guy named Jim Maguire."

"Why were you there?"

"Long story, got any Scotch?"

We settled in on the couch with my Scotch and her cabernet. I told her about the last two days, with very little emphasis on the Gabriella part.

When I finished, she was nodding. "You're excused for not coming to see me earlier. You've been a busy boy. You know, my husband played in Boca at a lounge owned by Lefty Rosenthal. Lefty was a genius at setting odds on sports events. All the big houses used him. I found him to be a real gentleman. He's not involved in that rough stuff, but I understand Boca is a destination for certain people."

"Know of anyone from Chicago named Pagano?"

"No, but the person you should ask about Chicago is your friend, Mimi, who owns the health food store. Her two husbands were from Chicago. One was an attorney, very politically connected, maybe more. That was a while ago, but she may still have friends there."

She stood and picked up my glass, "Freshen your drink?"

"Sure."

She turned toward the kitchen, then stopped. "This is a small town. I know the receptionist at Bingham Burroughs. Would you like me take her to lunch?

"No Kate, I don't want you getting involved."

She shrugged and continued to the kitchen, accentuating that little wiggle she knew I liked.

I'd always loved her body, the way it flowed when she walked. She didn't have much of a chest. I didn't care, the rest was magic.

It's interesting how much sexual desire is created in the imagination and how memories can relight that fire. Thoughts of the last night we were together came flooding back.

I got up and followed her into the kitchen.

I came up close behind her. She turned to face me and didn't back away. "That's not an 'I need another drink look'."

I answered with a big grin.

She put her glass on the kitchen counter, laced her arms around my neck, and gave me a long soft kiss. She took my hand and walked me down the hall to her bedroom. "Get comfortable, I'll be right back."

I sat on the edge of the bed, kicked off my shoes and socks, then stood again to take off the rest of my clothes. I was under the covers in no time, waiting and remembering. The softness of her skin, the passion in her kisses at the peak of our lovemaking, the sounds of her breathing, all there, neatly arranged in my memory.

Pictures of her kids at various ages, and of her two closest girl-friends covered the top of her dresser. They brought back other memories. Great kids, I thought. I'd known them when we were all a lot younger.

I heard her footsteps, then Sinatra from the den across the hall. "Fly me to the moon, let me play among the stars…" My mind drifted back to the soft skin. Nothing like an old friend with similar interests, I thought.

Suddenly the mood was broken. Her voice was high pitched, almost shrill. "Anthony, someone is out by your car!"

I jumped naked from the bed and ran to the living room. Sure enough, a car had stopped in front of the house. A man had gotten out from the passenger side. It was dark, but I'd swear it was Ryan. The driver had his window down. He was pointing, and saying something to the man on the street, checking out my car.

Kate had thrown on jeans and a sweater. "I'll go out. Ask them what they're looking for."

I grabbed her shoulder. "No, I'll go. It might be dangerous."

"For you, not me." She opened the door, which was on the side of the house, and stepped onto the lawn, still close to the door, but could be seen from the street.

"May I help you with something?" Her voice was surprisingly calm.

The driver was waving the other man back. He was saying something. Probably, "Get in the car."

It was a late model BMW, looked like a 750.

They sped off.

Kate ran into the street.

She came back in shaking her head. "Lights were out. I couldn't get the plate."

"Must have seen me talking to Mrs. Maguire." Big mistake, I thought. "They had to have followed me, and came back when they thought we'd be asleep. The stocky guy in the street, did you see his face?"

"Yes, crew cut, dark hair."

"Widow's peak?"

"Yup."

"That's Ryan, the guy I was telling you about."

"I don't like this, Anthony."

"I need to get out of here. I don't want you caught up in this."

I threw on my clothes and grabbed my keys from the table.

Kate was holding the door with one hand and grabbed my arm with the other. She kissed me on the cheek, and put her mouth to my ear. "Be careful, big guy. We've got some unfinished business."

I hesitated at the door imagining that unfinished business, but got into my car and drove back across the Southern Bridge.

Had someone seen the car leave Ryan's office? Had they guessed who I was at the funeral and followed me to my car? One thing was for sure for sure, the car had to go.

# Chapter 19

Back at the Brazilian there was a different kid on valet duty. I was going to ask him to keep an eye on the car, but didn't want to raise any suspicions.

I took the computer list from my room safe.

A little digging and there he was, James Maguire. He'd taken some money from his grandfather and started buying McDonald's franchises back in the Sixties. He owned about fifty. That's a lot of value.

My mind was racing with the possible scenarios. Had Maguire bought into the same deal as Frank? If he did, and the accident wasn't an accident, he must have bought it awhile ago and resold it to Pagano Inc., who was about to collect a big check.

The thought of Pagano made me realize that getting rid of the car wouldn't be enough. I needed another place. My guess was Tim Ryan wouldn't be anxious to tell Pagano he had been stupid enough to lose the list. His ass may be on the line if he didn't get it back. The list was a double–edged sword. I needed it to help Frank, but having it could get us both killed.

Maybe Sonja could find out who owned the BMW.

I was meeting Frank in the morning. His original suggestion to throw the computer list in the lake was looking better every hour.

The night seemed endless. Waking every two hours I added another worry, would they use Kate to get to me?

At four, I noticed the message light on my phone. The front desk had left a message about seven p.m. An envelope from Mrs. Fisher.

She had said she wanted to introduce me to Gabriella, hopefully that's what this was about. A pleasant thought, but not one to help me sleep.

Finally I slept. When I woke, the clock said 7:30. I was groggy, but still guessing at Mrs. Fisher's note.

I picked up her note, poured a coffee, black, and sat with Mrs. Fisher's letter.

Dear Anthony,

Gabriella Giacometti will be at my home on Tuesday evening. Hope you will attend. Cocktails at 7:00. Harriet

PS: My apologies for such short notice. At my age, we never plan more than a few days ahead.

I had to smile, age ninety and still that great sense of humor. She's on track for one-hundred.

I knew they'd be looking for me, but probably didn't know my connection to Frank. I still had time to walk the mile to Green's. Ryan would be watching for my car.

Green's wasn't crowded. Frank was at a table by the window reading the *New York Times*. He barely looked up as I settled in across from him.

"You're kind of quiet, Frank. Get lucky last night?"

He folded the paper, placed it on the vacant chair and gave me his pat line. "When it comes to women, all I've got is luck. There definitely is no skill involved."

He folded his big wrinkled hands on the table. "The answer is not just no, but no and I don't care. Truth is I miss Helena. By the time that feeling's passed I'll be too old to chase after anyone. She was twelve years younger than me. I was sure she'd outlive me."

I felt sad for my old buddy. We sat for a minute. Deb, our waitress took the order. She was excited. Her daughter had hit her fourth home run of the season.

I turned back to Frank. "Sounds like the art show was a bust."

He finally smiled. "The show was fine. I went with a friend of a friend. Attractive woman, but you'd think after all these years I'd know better. First, she dropped the names of a dozen politicians, movie stars, and prominent families, and how much they love her. Then I got, in spades, how wealthy the two ex-husbands were and how much they still adored her. Everyone she met got the kiss-kiss, hug-hug, 'love you' bit. And the, 'You must be so mad at me, I haven't called.' It was tedious."

I broke in. "I went to a wake for James Maguire last night. Your favorite insurance guy was there."

I had his attention. "What! Jay's dead? He's the one that introduced me to this guy Ryan at the seminar."

"You knew him?"

"Thirty years' worth of knowing him. What happened?"

"The paper said an accident."

"He got his policy long before I did. You think his policy had something to do with it?"

He answered his own question. "No. If Ryan were involved he wouldn't have been at the funeral."

I shook my head, "If he stayed away it might have aroused suspicion. Plus, when Ryan sold him, he could have met the wife. Doesn't mean she knew about the policy, or, if she did, who bought it. Besides, probably were other clients there. Good PR."

"Possible. Other than discussing how much she spent, Jay wasn't the type that involved his wife in his business."

Frank grew quiet. I know he was wondering the same thing I was.

He didn't say it aloud, only, "Where's the wake?"

"Tollman's, off Southern. You know it?"

"I'll go tonight." He gave me that stern look. "What else aren't you telling me?"

It was uncanny the way he could read people, me in particular.

"I stopped at Kate's. Two guys in a fairly new 750 were checking out my car. They must have seen me at Tollman's talking to Mrs. Maguire, wondered who I was."

"Tony! Tony! You're supposed to be a smart boy. If you were Ryan, trying to find who had stolen your papers, wouldn't you check out any new faces at a wake for a guy on the list?"

"You're right. I screwed up."

"I told you to get rid of that car. They're probably sitting out in the parking lot as we speak, waiting for you to come out."

"No. I walked."

"Well, that's one thing you did right. I'm going to meet Ryan for lunch. After I bought I referred him to a couple of friends. I'm still licensed. He knows I could have asked him for a commission split and didn't. Maybe I can find some answers before he connects us."

He looked up at me. "So what else aren't you telling me?"

"That I'll be playing golf Thursday with Jay's daughter, Jennifer."

"How'd you work that?" He seemed excited.

Finally, I thought, a little recognition for something done right. I pretended I was curling the ends of my mustache. "I have my ways."

He stood up. "She's a good one. She and her father were close. She may know things his wife doesn't. She may have her own ideas on whether it was more than an accident."

He slapped me on the back. "Don't get run over by that BMW before you get to play golf."

I stood and held out my palms. "Frankie. I grew up in the North End. I hung out with kids that became 'made guys.' I can certainly jump out of the way of a BMW."

It sounded good. I hoped I wouldn't have to.

# Chapter 20

As I entered my room, my cell was ringing. Sonja. She had checked on the BMW. Palm Beach has a very high-tech police force. Every car that comes into town has its license plate picked up on camera and fed into a computer. Before they get from one side of the bridge to the other, the police know if the car is stolen, leased, or whatever. This car didn't belong to Tim Ryan. It was leased to a company in Boca. She couldn't get anything on the company, probably a shell.

She didn't consider that good news, and neither did I.

I called the front desk for a cab, told them I was leaving town for a couple of days, and to leave my room as is. I packed a small bag, put on the jacket and slacks I needed for cocktails at Mrs. Fisher's, and took the cab to the airport.

From the airport, I took another cab to the Jaguar dealer and rented another car, a bright red convertible. I knew Frank's comment would be a classic. "I see you're in hiding, Tony. Nice job!" or something close. I hoped they'd be looking for me in the car I'd left at the Brazilian.

I'd spend a few days at the Marriott at City Place, but first, I decided to take Kate's advice and visit Mimi, Palm Beach's "Medicine Woman."

Every day, dozens of Palm Beach residents come to Mimi's little store on Royal Poinciana with ailments — actual or anticipated. Standing behind her narrow counter, Mimi is a poster girl for her cures. You wouldn't believe someone who is old enough to have been a teenager in Paris when World War II started could spend eight hours a day climbing stepladders and standing at a counter dispensing advice, but seventeen years teaching yoga, and a lifetime of living what she preaches, has kept her body and mind young.

Each inquiry receives a nod, a knowing smile, and a raised index finger. Then in very proper English, "Yes, I have just the thing." She leaves the counter, climbs a small ladder, and soon is holding just the right bottle, box, or jar while explaining its benefits in detail. Her thousands of homeopathic concoctions are certain to cure everything from common colds to missing organs. Clients leave with a smile and the assurance that other Palm Beach customers have sworn by this remedy.

When I spent longer periods in Palm Beach I was a regular. My daily fare was organic carrot juice with wheat grass and a shot of ginseng. If she had time to chat, I'd stay. We'd talk about life in general, but hers was particularly interesting. As a child she lived in a penthouse in Paris where the building owner's best friend, one Pablo Picasso, had painted murals on the walls. Her family's servants were members of the royal family who had fled the 1918 Russian Revolution. They cooked, cleaned, and chauffeured her family about the city.

She wouldn't say much about her former career as a top New York model, but she could talk forever about literature, her years living in Europe, and my favorite, the Palm Beach of the past, when parties with movie stars and the rich and famous were her daily fare.

Today I was looking for something else. Since one of her two

Chicago husbands had been politically connected and possibly had some association with the Mob, I wanted her help scouting out Gabriella's probable employer, Mr. Pagano, the waste-disposal guy. Hopefully I could determine if waste was the only thing he disposed of.

Mimi was enthusiastically explaining the antioxidant powers gained from green/white tea to two middle-aged women. I walked to the back of the store where the carrots are juiced and chatted with the nice Jamaican woman in the juice bar until Mimi was free.

I didn't want to reveal too much, but had a feeling she'd be of help. As I paid for the juice, I asked, "Does your ex-husband still live in Chicago?"

She usually has the reserved demeanor of a woman of her era, with the hint of a smile, as though something has just reminded her of an interesting tale. My question brought an unexpected blank stare. Then she slowly cocked her head to one side, and broke into a wide grin.

"What in the world would prompt you to ask such a thing?"

I owed her an explanation, but didn't feel I should get too specific.

"I have a friend who may have some problems with fellows in the waste management business in Chicago. I'd like to help him get it resolved."

"I had two ex-husbands from Chicago. They both died years ago." As an afterthought she added, "I was courted by wealthy older men in those days."

She stopped, then in a slower more deliberate voice she continued. "So Mr. Tauck, a friend with a problem. Well yes, my ex-husband's son is an attorney in Chicago. He took over his father's practice. Just what is your friend's issue?"

I could tell she was mocking my "I have a friend" excuse when she emphasized the word "friend."

"Do you have contact with him?"

"Yes I do. He is very respectful of his old stepmother. We correspond on holidays and he comes here once a year for a week. Usually stays at the Breakers. I get together for dinner with him and his wife, a lovely woman."

I continued on with what Mimi clearly knew was a charade. "My friend needs to know about a fellow named Pagano. Vitorio Pagano."

"Oh my," she said. "You mean the mobster?" She looked around to see if anyone was within earshot. "I've met Vitorio, through my husband. In those days, politicians and the underworld, which was our term for the Mob, were often quite close."

"This Vitorio, what was he like?"

She gave me a full smile, but her eyes narrowed. It looked like she might laugh, but I feared she wouldn't.

"Now Anthony," she began. Once again raising that index finger, but now tipping her head back slightly, "You have been coming to my store for years. You never discuss your business with me, which I respect. Now you want me to get involved. What is this all about?"

I don't know why I thought a ploy as old as "I have a friend" would hold water with someone of her experience, so I decided tell her the story, leaving out Gabriella and the papers in my car. Occasionally we were interrupted by customers. Mimi was fascinated.

I finished by wondering aloud whether Vitorio Pagano may have had people killed to speed up the collection process.

"Well, that is quite a tale. I only met Mr. Pagano on two occasions and that was many years ago, but I did speak with him at length both times. He was born in Italy and is very into his Italian heritage. He spent a lot of time there, was a collector of Italian Art and had homes in Milan and Switzerland. I think Davos. I found it fascinating that this outwardly cultured man could have this other, exceptionally dangerous side."

She hesitated for a moment, and put her hand to her forehead. "Another thing, he was a ski instructor as a young man and one of the most handsome and charming men I have ever met."

I nodded. Even his most recent newspaper photos showed this.

Mimi continued, "He was an intriguing character, but having people killed to collect on insurance policies would be too crude for him. I don't suggest he never had anyone 'bumped off,' as they say." She laughed at herself, for using a slang expression. "But if he's involved in this scheme, it is much more complex than you're imagining."

I thanked her and drove to the Marriott.

# Chapter 21

My corner room on the Marriott's tenth floor had a small balcony over the front door facing Okeechobee. To the east I could see the Kravis Center and City Place, both part of the ten-year-old urban renewal project that had revitalized West Palm Beach.

I called the front desk, hoping for a quick lesson on how to use the room's computer. Fortunately, the very engaging young woman on duty picked up on my ignorance and asked what I was trying to accomplish. She guided me into the City Hall records for obituaries.

With the computer printout of Palm Beach's first families, I began the search to match my list with deaths recorded at City Hall.

A match didn't necessarily mean they had bought coverage. Some would have refused to see Ryan at all, and others would have been rejected for poor health. Frank had to get Ryan to tell him who among the matching names he'd insured.

The first match came quickly. "Jacob Aston, longtime resident of Palm Beach, died March third after a long illness. He was eighty-seven. He leaves his wife, Helen, of 47 years, and three children…, etc."

Puzzled, I read it again "after a long illness." Usually that means cancer. Vitorio Pagano from Chicago doesn't use long illnesses to rub people out. Aston wouldn't have been able to get coverage.

I looked for more matches and got as far back as April, just about a year. It was 11:10. I needed to reach Frank before his lunch with Tim Ryan. Out of one hundred and fifty deaths in the Palm Beach area, three more were on the list, all wealthy men and all died of various health issues. None were accidents.

I called Frank's cell. He hates cell phones and keeps his in his car. I hoped he had it turned on.

I was lucky. "Frankie, when are you meeting your guy for lunch?"

"12:30 at Cucina. Don't show up."

"Very funny. I found four people on the list that died in the last five months, all were natural causes, cancer, heart type things. Try and find out if any of them were insured by Ryan, and if he resold their policies."

"Tony, I have a little leverage with this guy, but he's not going to tell me everything. I'll find out what I can. Give me the names."

I gave him Aston and the three others. One was in his late seventies the rest all mid eighties.

I hung up, and went back to matching the list to the obituaries. I got back to a year from last September and the matches stopped. There were only two more over the prior year, six total, plus James Maguire.

My cell rang. It was Frank. "Tony, where are you?"

"Still at the Marriott, did you find anything out?"

"Yes, I told him I was concerned about his selling my policy to someone who might profit from my being dead. Then I told him I'd been checking the obituaries for Palm Beach and had found ten prominent people in my age group who died in the last eighteen months. I read the names and asked if he'd insured any of them."

"I only gave you four."

"I added a few more to my list so he wouldn't get suspicious. He'd insured three of the four you gave me. The first guy Aston, and two others."

"What else did he say?"

"He said all three had been insured for awhile. I had to push the little turd on this one. He didn't want to tell me if they had sold their policies. He was pretty evasive. I got the impression they all had. He also avoided their cause of death."

"No problem. We can guess cause of death from the obituaries. But, Frank, isn't it strange, all four died of illness, no accidents? Some were long illnesses and they'd only had the policy three or four years. How did they get coverage?"

"Yeah, it is strange they're not dying of accidents. Maybe we're off base."

I asked, "Were they all written through the same insurance company?"

"I think they're all with the company that I bought: Gibraltar. That was Ryan's main company when he was a broker. It's one of the largest companies in the business. Good stock to buy, Tony."

"Course it's a good stock, these guys are selling insurance up the ying-yang. Wait till the real claims come in. Course, the guys running the company will have made their money and retired rich. Later, someone else will pay the fiddler."

"Sounds from what you've found that they already are. Ryan says I'll make a nice profit. He was trying to avoid the fact that some of the guys who bought the same policy as me have died. They'd have made out better if they'd kept the coverage themselves. The group that bought these policies made out like bandits."

"Nice job, Frankie. I thought your memory was going?"

"It is. Last night I climbed into the shower with my glasses on. Next it'll be my pants. Listen close. Get the story quick. By tonight, I'll have forgotten I had lunch, let alone who with and what we discussed."

"Frankie," I laughed, "You've been complaining about this for years. Let me give you a test. When was the last time you had sex?"

"Two weekends ago, why?"

"What happened?"

"Well," he began, "Younger sister of an old girl friend in town called me. We ended up at my place. Her hearing aid fell out. She didn't realize how much noise she was making. Nearly woke up the whole neighborhood."

"Frankie. Your memory is fine!"

We laughed, and then I noticed the time. "I got to get ready. We'll talk tomorrow."

"Tony, one more thing. There is an advantage to being my age."

"What's that Frank?"

"When you fall asleep after sex, they don't get mad. They give you a kiss on the forehead and let you be."

# Chapter 22

I put on my blue blazer, white pants, and favorite tie. It has a light blue and turquoise background under a gold and purple mesh in the shape of sea shells. It's kind of hard for a guy to describe, but women seem to like it. I was hoping Gabriella would like it, and me. Fact is, as I drove down Mrs. Fisher's long, hedge-lined driveway, just thinking Gabriella would be there made me a little nervous. I never get nervous, but I was.

I thought I was on time, but half a dozen cars were already waiting to be parked. Three valets were running back and forth parking them on the side lawn. Other cars were dropping off passengers and returning to their own modest estates. Dinner parties in Palm Beach are not what you and I might call intimate.

I was greeted by Harold, who ushered me in with an attractive couple, whose names I failed to catch. The party was on the back patio and the lawn overlooking the lake.

Before descending the three steps to the yard, I stopped on the landing to, as we say in my business, case the crowd.

Mrs. Fisher stood below me to the right, greeting guests and making introductions. Sure enough, straight ahead was my former mother-in-law, stiff as ever. She was engaged in conversation with a young couple and actually sporting a half smile. The couple and their grandparents had to be members of the Everglades and Bath and Tennis. No one lesser rates her hello, let alone a smile.

I felt a sense of sadness for my ex-wife. When we'd met she'd exuded a warmth and kindness for everyone. Her mother had always resented her sweetness, and after our marriage she seemed to resent her happiness, too. The mother had squeezed the joy out of Elizabeth like you squeeze the juice from a lemon, until she finally mirrored her mother's sour look.

My thoughts of better times with my ex-wife were interrupted by a gentle touch on my elbow.

"Excuse me. You seem to be surveying the crowd. Have you seen our hostess?" The voice had a slight Italian accent, but the English was perfect.

I turned and was face to face with a smiling Gabriella.

"Let me guess, Northern Italy, Milano."

Her eyes sparkled at the chance for repartee. "I am a citizen of the world, but you are almost correct. I spent my childhood in Davos and have spent much time in Milano. You are?"

"Anthony Tauck from Boston, an unworldly citizen of the States, but a frequent visitor to Milano."

"I am Gabriella Giacometti, so pleasant to meet you, Mr. Tauck."

"Giacometti, like my favorite sculptor?"

She held out the perfectly manicured hand I had so admired in the mirror at the Palm Beach Grill. Her hand fit naturally into mine and was as warm and soft as I had imagined. The handshake was business-like, but her eyes had a look of recognition, and there was a hint of flirtatiousness in her smile. Was this her natural look, or directed at just me? Had she recognized me from the Grill and Ralph Lauren?

"Alberto Giacometti was my…"

Her escort, whom I recognized from our encounter at Ralph Lauren, had been standing behind her during this exchange. He moved in beside her, put his arm about her waist and led her away, "Come. I see Mrs. Fisher. We must pay our respects."

I pointed. "Yes, Harriet is right over there."

Noting his annoyance at my too-familiar reference to Mrs. Fisher, Gabriella looked back and smiled. She showed little resistance to being led away, but sent a shoulder shrug in my general direction.

Must be George Bingham. I wondered why a woman that strong would allow herself to be controlled in such a way. Is it her Italian upbringing or maybe how she retains actual control?

I watched as Gabriella and Bingham approached their hostess. George seemed reluctant to interrupt, almost fawning, whereas Gabriella was showing the respect Mrs. Fisher's years deserved, but otherwise talking to her as an equal. I wondered again what her real relationship with George could be. I thought about Mrs. Fisher's words, "She should be with you." I had to agree, but what could I do to make that happen? Gabriella had been in the middle of a sentence with me, when Bingham jerked her away. Without some serious luck, it wasn't going to happen at this party.

Somewhat comfortable in the knowledge that she should be with me, I headed to the large oval bar.

The white-jacketed bartender handed me a Dewar's on the rocks. As I turned, a tall stick-like fellow with a thick patch of sandy hair clicked his champagne glass against mine.

"Fine party, eh chap? Don't recognize you as a regular. Do you know anyone here?"

I couldn't tell if his accent was a generation from being pure British or Palm Beach acquired, and wondered if he was questioning whether I belonged in this August group. A wide smile, accentuated by a small mole about a third of the way across his upper lip, dispelled any negative thoughts.

I clicked my glass against his. "So far I know three people. Mrs. Fisher, my ex-mother-in-law, whom I don't care to talk to, and one other woman I'd love to talk to.

He laughed, "I know most of these people, same faces at every party. This town is divided into fairly specific groups, the Everglades/Bath & Tennis group, the newly rich, the international set, and a few other smaller sects sometimes divided by nationality. They know each other from Manhattan, the Hampton's and Palm Beach. Each group often keeps to themselves. Mrs. Fisher's parties are a little more democratic than most. She invites outsiders, those whose only claim to fame is they are smart and interesting. I take it you are one of those. Let me give you a rundown of some of the regulars." He put his hand on my shoulder and turned me slightly to the left. "See that handsome blonde fellow over there in the blazer and ascot? Hasn't a penny. Got lucky and married that rather large pink woman with the big hair."

I laughed. "You and I have a different definition of luck."

"They both got what they wanted. He wanted a big house and parties like this. She wanted a handsome escort."

He pointed his drink at a well-dressed gentleman in a seersucker suit and open collar who was having an argument with an attractive blonde. She appeared a little tipsy. "Those two have an interesting life. They live in an estate on the water with two maids, a chef, a chauffeur, and a bookkeeper-manager. All day long the woman plays backgammon on the Internet with people she doesn't know. He reads the newspapers in the morning, and works out every afternoon with a personal trainer. All day, they don't eat. At about four he starts sipping, so that when she comes down at five he'll feel mellow enough to deal with her. By about six he's still OK, but she's in the wrapper. By seven they're in a vicious argument over dinner. Between them there are six children and five marriages. Only one of the children communicates in any way, unless maybe a trust fund check is late." He raised his glass again. "Here's to money, the root of all evil."

He nodded toward a tall, very thin, probably once real blonde. "Her husband was caught kissing the minister. She spends a lot of time in Bible study groups, I assume trying to figure life out." He hesitated, and then looked heavenward, "Or maybe figuring death out. You would think a minister trying to steal her husband would have turned her off to religion, but what do I know?"

While enjoying his monologue, I was searching the crowd for Gabriella, my main reason for being there. No luck. Any time I spotted her, George was hovering.

My friend nodded toward a woman with a slim, but shapely figure, black shoulder length hair, and the strut of a runway model. She was maneuvering her way though the crowd toward the bar. "This lady hired the wrong actuary."

I gave him a quizzical look. "She hired an actuary?" Did he know who I was?

He continued. "She courted, if that's the correct expression, maybe flirted is better, her way into a marriage with a very rich seventy-nine-year old. After ten long years, she gave up waiting for him to either die or lose his virility, and took a divorce. He's now ninety-three and going strong. Those ten years were his fountain of youth."

I nodded, "She should have gotten his medical records, and then seen an actuary. Course actuaries need lots of numbers for statistical probabilities, which means she'd have needed several husbands to guarantee at least one early death."

"I like your thinking. You'd be good at this game."

As the object of his discussion approached the bar, my new friend greeted her with a hug, and then, holding her at arm's length, said, "Tamara, how is the husband-hunting business?"

She shrugged, "I'm holding out for you, Emile. Why don't you quit chasing those twenty-year-olds and find out what a real woman is like?"

He laughed, "I go young, knowing love is as temporary as life."

Then, nodding toward Tamara, he winked at me, "Unfortunately, not always temporary enough."

She nodded to the bartender as though she knew him. He handed her a flute of Dom Perignon.

"Emile darling, enough fun at my expense, you didn't introduce me to your friend. He's good-looking, but too young to outlive. Maybe he has a rich father I can marry."

I'd gotten into Emile's game and had been her watching closely. Her nose was long and narrow, pointed at the end. The effect made me think at first, she might be cross-eyed. This was not the case at all. When I examined her again, eyes, nose, mouth, the total package was quite striking.

I held out my hand, "Tony Tauck. No rich father, but nice to make your acquaintance." Her nails were a bright red, matching her lipstick. Her hands, very white and soft were supporting several rings, one a diamond the size of a skating rink. The deep blue eyes made me wonder if she had pulled a reversal on the typical Palm Beach blonde and dyed her hair black. Her handshake was weak, which surprised me, considering the weight of her jewelry. Her mouth was another story.

"A pleasure to meet you, Tony Tauck. I take it you're a friend of Harriet's. How do you know her?" Then she stopped. "Oh, I guess that's not fair. I should tell you first. Harriet is a friend and contemporary of my ex-husband's. I'm sure that Emile, sometimes known as 'the public broadcasting service', has probably already told you my story." She gave Emile a fake smile, and took a sip of champagne, "I love Harriet; she's a darling woman, so open and non-judgemental. If you've got the goods as a person, she's your friend, dough or no dough."

She didn't need to know the real story behind how I knew Harriet. "I met her through my friend Frank Forbes, many years ago. Yes, she's very special."

We had moved away from the bar to make room for the crowd when Emile leaned toward me and whispered, "Don't look now, but there's a very attractive woman checking you out."

Tamara, who was facing the bar, had noticed as well. She cupped her hand so no one could read her lips. "Emile, she's with that nasty George Bingham." She waved and called out. "George! George darling, don't try to ignore me. Come right over here and bring your gorgeous friend."

That was my excuse to turn around. I tried to focus on George, who was leading Gabriella through the crowd, but I had trouble not staring. To most men my age, Sophia Loren represents the perfect woman. Gabriella had the same full lips and smile, plus all that other stuff we like about Sophia.

"Hello, I'm George Bingham," was directed at me, and brought me out of my reverie. Definitely the same guy Gabriella was with in Ralph Lauren, tall and, in spite of a slouch, his narrow shoulders made him look even taller. Expecting a continuation of his negative reaction to my calling Mrs. Fisher Harriet, I tried to neutralize him. I held out a hand and smiled. "Anthony Tauck. Isn't your name on the masthead of a very prominent law firm? What's your specialty?"

He seemed taken back by the question. His narrow face became even narrower as he took on his serious demeanor. "Yes, the firm was started by my grandfather. I have no direct specialty. My practice generally follows the needs of our clients."

Gabriella, who had been listening, grabbed George by the arm. "He's so modest. George is a brilliant attorney specializing in tax law."

George, entranced, smiled uncomfortably.

Tamara, sensing my interest in Gabriella, grabbed George by the arm and led him away. "George darling, where have you been keeping yourself?"

I found myself alone with Gabriella and wasn't sure for how long. I launched quickly into my well-rehearsed spiel. "Giacometti is one of my favorites. Is that your married or maiden name?"

She looked up at me with those big brown eyes and slowly parted her lips into a full smile. "Your favorite sculptor was my grandfather. Which of his pieces do you admire most?" Her eyes grew cautious, the smile was gone. Clearly men had used that line before.

Thankfully I had done my homework. "I'm fascinated by his mental block as a young man which prevented him from sculpting anything bigger than his thumb. Do you own any of his miniatures?"

The smile returned. "They're on exhibit in Venice, but that was a very early period, before he broke with his father and left home."

"Do you remember him as a child?"

She laughed, and fluttered her eye lids. "Well Mr. Tauck, you are as Harriet said, a very interesting man. First you were checking my marital status, now you're fishing for my age, and we've barely met."

Seeing that George was engaged by Tamara and Emile, I moved closer and put my hand on her bare shoulder. "Like Sophia Loren, you are ageless."

Then, in case she felt I was too forward, I continued the conversation on her grandfather. "Seriously, I am fascinated by Giacometti's life. For example, his inability to settle down. How did he raise a family? Spend time with his grandchildren?"

"To answer your questions, grandfather died when I was ten. He was as passionate about his grandchildren as his art, and I was fortunate to have had him in my life."

I realized that all this time my hand was on her shoulder she had not pulled away. I was finally feeling more relaxed and wanted to keep our conversation going. "Do you paint or sculpt?"

"No, but my name is perhaps why I deal in art. People always assumed I would end up in this field, so I became what they expected. This happens to many of us, don't you agree?"

"Yes, but I think there is more to it than that. People don't buy art based on your grandfather's reputation. I was told by Harriet that you are exceptional at what you do."

She shrugged, but was not uncomfortable with the compliment. She looked down, and was silent for a moment. "I think of my family often, though they are all gone now."

I was a little surprised she didn't react to my mention that Mrs. Fisher had spoken of her, but moved closer as she continued. "My mother passed away a year ago. Our memories take up so much of our day. How little of our time is spent in the present, so much mingling of past and future." I slid my hand slowly down her upper arm before I removed it.

Gabriella smiled the relaxed smile of a woman who knows her power and is comfortably in charge.

I glanced over at my co-conspirators who were in lively conversation with George. Emile must have guessed Gabriella was the third person I had referred to. He turned briefly from George and held up two fingers in a peace sign. I smiled and nodded back.

Gabriella glanced over, and continued to talk about her grandfather.

Knowing time was limited, I broke in, "How did you come to meet Harriet?"

"I have some experience in Italian art and Harriet has an interest in collecting. George was nice enough to make the introduction. His firm manages her affairs."

Harriet had said they'd met at a dinner party. Maybe George had arranged the meeting. Possibly he was shrewder than I'd been told.

I was thinking about our two former "near meetings" and how much she had haunted my thoughts. If she had been thinking of me it didn't show.

Suddenly she surprised me.

She looked me straight in the eye and gave me her best smile. "Harriet told me what you do, and said I could trust you. I would like to see you again on a different matter." She handed me her card. Without looking away, I put it in my shirt pocket. We stood silently for a long moment before she spoke. "George is a little boy, but he has been very kind to me. I must go to him. Call me tonight. I'll have him take me straight home from the party."

She turned and called out, "George, you've been ignoring me."

He looked like he might blush at the attention. She grabbed his arm and they headed for the buffet along the wall by the lake.

So much of the fire in a new relationship builds in the mind between meetings. For me, the match was struck with our eye contact in the Grill, small coals began to glow when we almost met in Ralph Lauren, and now after talking, touching, and being asked to a mysterious meeting, I was ready for a full scale conflagration. Was she?

Emile gave the bartender a nod to refresh my Dewar's.

"Well Tony, I must say, I'm impressed by your choice in women. I'd gladly give up a couple of twenty-five-year-olds for a shot at that fifty-year-old."

Not wanting to seem excited, I muttered. "Yes, she's very nice."

"That's an understatement," said Emile. "Talk about Intelligent Design!"

"Thanks to you and Tamara, I got a chance to talk."

"Tamara hates George. He was advising her husband against her."

"So she never got the money?"

"No, no, her husband was very generous to her, probably still supports her. They had an understanding. It worked well for both; she just wasn't planning on it lasting that long."

He stopped, and then smiled. "I think he lied about his health. Well, back to our game. See that fellow over there?"

He was pointing toward a very dapper older gentleman in a tan suit and straw hat, sporting a pencil moustache.

"He is said to have killed his third wife, just before their divorce was finalized. Apparently she was going to take him to the cleaners. It was never proven. Interesting fellow nonetheless."

It was clear that Emile's knowledge of the community might be of help, but my thoughts were in another place. I fingered her card in my shirt pocket. It had her name, no address, and what looked like a Delray phone number. Delray is a small, fast growing town, about fifteen miles south. I could get there in about thirty minutes. Best to meet her there, I thought. The buffet looked tempting, but I needed time to sort things out before I called.

Emile was still talking; I was half listening. Gabriella had clearly sought me out at the bar. When we met coming in, she knew who I was, and had obviously discussed me at length with Harriet. What this all meant remained to be seen.

I put my unfinished drink on the bar and shook Emile's hand. "Thanks for your help, Emile. Do you have a card?"

He pulled it out quickly. "Call me, we'll do lunch at the Sail Fish Club."

I turned it over. Emile DuPont.

"I will. Thanks again, Emile."

Trying not to make eye contact and risk delay, I hurried for the door.

# Chapter 23

Back at the Marriott, I called Frank and told him of my conversation with Gabriella.

Frank was ready for combat. "Tony, what is it with you and women? There's no middle ground. You're either 'The Man' or a shrinking violet. With this Gabriella, I'm thinking the color purple. Do you really think she's an innocent little lamb? She's involved with some very bad people. She's dating George, who's probably the link between the list and the trash guy from Chicago. She's playing George like a fiddle, and you think she's not playing you? Get a grip."

I was searching for a reply when he continued, "Her loyalties are to Pagano. He's dangerous and may know you have a computer list that could be very incriminating.

I didn't want to hear it. "But Frank, she told Harriet she had a problem, and Harriet told her to talk to me. Why would she do that if she wants me dead?"

"Tony, you're not listening. Once Pagano knows about the list, you're in his sights — and she's the bullet. You're being set up."

I knew Frank was right. My desire to connect with Gabriella was clouding my judgment and distracting me from helping Frank.

"Tony, I don't think you should go down there at all, especially not alone."

I hung up and called Harriet to confirm Gabriella's story. Someone I didn't recognize answered. "Mrs. Fisher is not available. She is with her guests."

I took a deep breath and sat for a minute. Rational thought was not in the cards, only the images of those lips and slow smile, those legs, and how great they looked walking away.

I took out her card and dialed.

"Gabriella, it's Tony."

"Oh yes, Anthony. May we meet?"

Her English, with its inflection, clearly sounded private school. When I didn't respond she continued.

"There is a bistro on the main street of Delray called 32 East. Can you be there at eleven?"

"Yes. Will you be alone?"

"Of course, why would you ask?"

"No reason." I hesitated. "I mean, if you are speaking with someone, should I wait and approach you alone?"

I wasn't sure how direct I should be with her. I started again slowly, "What I meant to say is that if you have a problem, should we be seen together? Some people know what I do."

"I will be alone."

I wondered again how she might be interpreting our relationship. Men often think of flirting as foreplay. Unfortunately for us men, for most women, it doesn't count. In my mind we had exchanged more than looks at the Grill, communicated in Ralph Lauren, connected by proxy through Harriet, and touched and spoke today. In my mind we had gone on the equivalent of at least two dates. Where was she? Probably mulling over the idea of a first date.

# Chapter 24

The ride down A1A, the coast road, is normally slow. Lots of speed traps and radar on this winding ride through estates, high-rise condos, golf and beach clubs, and single-family communities. I turned right at the Marriott on to Atlantic, the main street into Delray. My thoughts on our meeting ranged from being tortured and killed, to spending the night making love. There were no in-betweens.

The ride had gone too quickly. I stepped into 32 East, before I had even formulated a "what if" plan.

I stood in the doorway for a full thirty seconds, until the heavy crowd gently pushed me inside. I found myself at the end of a bar, which ran nearly the entire length of the building. A short wooden railing separated the bar crowd from the almost vacant dining room. I picked my way though the empty tables, surveying the room for Gabriella and for what else, I wasn't sure. From the preponderance of jackets on the men, it appeared most couples had finished dinner and were staying for after-dinner drinks. I made a mental note to add this place to my list of comfortable hangouts. I was beginning to feel I'd been stood up, or worse, set up, when I spotted a row of booths beyond the bar. She must be back there, I thought. Four men were playing cards in the first booth. No one looked like

Mafia. In the next booth sat a woman in sweats and a loose sweater, a Dolphins cap pulled low on her forehead. Gabriella.

I looked around; the last booth was empty. There was an emergency exit beyond the booths. It was unlocked and led to a wide, dimly lit alley. Everything seemed normal other than my slight nervousness about the card players.

Satisfied, I folded myself into the booth opposite Gabriella. In the dim light her olive skin looked darker than I remembered, her eyes more green than brown. She sat with her hands folded carefully on the table between us. No jewelry, just a light tan on soft smooth skin. Cap, sweater, sweats, no matter, my imagination knew what they were hiding.

For a moment Gabriella didn't speak, as though she were struggling over how to start. What came was unexpected.

"Well, Mr. Tauck, tell me, was that not you undressing me in the mirror at the Palm Beach Grill? Seems a little crude for a man of your age, don't you think?" Her tone was cold; she wasn't smiling.

In an instant, all my fantasies of the last three days crashed and burned. I felt my face flush. "Embarrassed fool" had to be written all over it. Not knowing how to reply, I glanced toward the dining area looking for an escape route.

When I looked back, she was doubled over with laughter. She reached across the table and took my hand. "Sorry, that was mean." Her eyes twinkled as she slowly watched me regain my composure.

"I just wanted to see if you had a guilty conscience."

She sensed my discomfort, and gave my hand a gentle squeeze.

"Mrs. Fisher said you had spent time in Milano?"

Still not fully recovered, I stammered, "I have, I mean I do. I go there two, three times a year. Why?"

The full smile that I'd come to love spread across her face. "My girlfriend and I were watching you. She said the way you were looking at me, if we were in Milano, I'd be sore from your pinches."

She had set me up, but now she'd broken the ice. I thought of Frank's warning, "I think she's setting you up," and smiled ruefully.

When we had talked at the party, I'd sensed a hint of vulnerability. It was gone. Could she turn it on and off at will, I wondered?

I thought of her words, "George is a little boy, but he has been kind to me." I hoped she didn't think of me as just another man, so easy to manipulate.

She interrupted my thoughts. "Harriet told me you're an insurance detective. Just what is the background for that position?"

Trying to figure if this was the reason she had wanted to meet, I thought for a minute, then decided on how to answer in a way she'd understand.

"My grandfather was a detective on the Boston police. I grew up wanting to be like him, but instead spent ten years selling life insurance. Then, by luck, I got a chance to do both. A man bought a large policy on his employer and planned to kill her for the proceeds. I discovered what was going on and prevented it. That got me started, and the calls kept coming."

Her knowing look made me wonder if Mrs. Fisher had told her my story. I smiled and continued. "The ability to read people and situations is a key to success. As you can see, I'm not real good at that part."

She had let go of my hand, now took it again. "It was unfair to tease you that way. What is it you are investigating now? Are you allowed to tell me?"

Wow! She sure knew how to get to the point, but what to tell her?

I decided to talk about Frank, hoping I could flush out what she knew about Bingham and Pagano.

"Competition sometimes pushes insurance premiums down to a level where policies are a very good investment. When this occurs companies buy policies on elderly people and hold for the return at death, which is favorable."

I was about to tell her my friend had a policy, but she interrupted. "Others realize this and buy the policies." Her voice was flat, as though I were confirming something she hoped wasn't true.

But then she got specific. She lifted her eyes to meet mine and asked, "Are you investigating death claims on older people in Palm Beach?"

The question was so direct, it disarmed me. "Yes, I am. My friend Frank has a policy, and I'm interested in protecting him."

She seemed relieved. "So you don't work for a company?"

"No. Not at all."

She slid out from her side of the booth and held out her hand. "Come. I want to show you something."

We left through the back door, walked swiftly down the alley to a side street and turned east toward the ocean. Two blocks further we arrived at a small condominium building with, maybe, six units. Hers was on the first floor. She turned the key, ushered me inside, clicked on a couple of lights, and double-locked the door.

She motioned to the large couch. "Sit here."

The room was sparsely decorated with very heavy, dark, probably mahogany, furniture. From my seat in the living room I could see a large table in the dining room stacked with art books and clothing samples. For selecting the Mafia don's new suits, I assumed.

Before I could get up to explore, she came and sat close to me on the couch. On her lap she held a large scrapbook, which she opened to the first page. There was a black-and-white photo of a young girl with a broad smile standing between two men.

I pointed to the photo, "You?"

She smiled and nodded.

"What age?"

"I was five with my two favorite men, my father and my uncle."

I was curious but kept still. She had invited me to her home to explain some unknown danger. Why were we were looking over family photos?

To allow me a better view of the photos, she had moved the book to my lap, and leaned into me to point and comment as she turned the pages. I recognized a hint of lavender, the same subtle scent I smelled on the woman in the Palm Beach Grill. Feeling embolden, I slid my arm around her shoulder and placed it gently on her arm.

Her tone grew soft when describing the black-and-white prints of her and others with her grandfather. Slowly her book took us through time. We were looking at her as a teenager, beside one of the men from the first photo, when I asked, "What happened to the man in the earlier photos?"

That was my father. He died when I was ten, the same year as my grandfather. My grandfather was ill for several years. My father died a month after becoming ill with cancer. My uncle and my mother were close. He raised me as though I were his own daughter."

She would touch my arm or hand as she explained who people were. The photos were bringing back memories and feelings of family, an intimacy she somehow wanted me to share or at least understand. Through her tone and vivid descriptions of her family gatherings I began to recognize that honoring family and tradition was as natural to her as breathing. My Americanized Italian family, with cousins, uncles, and grandparents living in the same neighborhood, sharing meals may seem old-fashioned in today's transient society, but compared to Gabriella's my family was twenty-first century.

After looking through many photos of Gabriella at different stages of her life, I could see the gradual attrition to less family more friends. She stopped, leaned back against the couch and sat quietly, her eyes downcast. The importance of her album was clear. Everyone but her uncle, seen in so many of the black-and-white photos, was gone.

I gave her shoulder a squeeze. "Your uncle is your only surviving relative?"

She nodded slowly, then turned to face me. Her full red lips were only inches from mine. I had an overwhelming desire to kiss her, but there was something in her look that made me hesitate. It was as though she were looking into my soul to find trust. There was some secret she needed to share, something about her family, her uncle. I waited, but she turned back to the book.

We sat close, our hips, thighs and shoulders touching, as she continued to turn pages. Each page continued her story, school friends, ski trips to Switzerland, family holidays. Through her photos, she was showing me who she was. A woman defined by a family that now lived through her.

The warmth of her against me had again caused my thoughts to drift. Then it struck me. We were looking at a more recent photo of Gabriella being hugged by her uncle.

I recognized him from the articles in the *Chicago Tribune*. It was Vitorio Pagano. But I couldn't let her know I had done my homework. Was this album her way of telling me?

"What is this photo? You look so sad."

"That was me at mother's funeral, a year ago next month."

I had to push her. "Somehow he looks familiar."

"Yes, though he is a private person, he is often in the press. You know of Vitorio Pagano?"

"Yes, a little. Isn't he from Chicago?"

She laughed, "He lives in Chicago, but he is very much from Italy. He is my adopted uncle. From my photos you can tell we are very close. He's who I work for now." She pointed to samples on the table. "He's a fastidious dresser. I was having suits made for him of the most expensive linen available."

I wondered about the "was having" but didn't ask.

"You know him by a very different reputation than I. He is the reason I need your help."

I pulled my arm from her back and faced her on the couch.

"How could I possibly be of help to him?"

She took my hand and held it in her lap. "Not to him, Anthony, to me."

"I don't understand."

She looked away. "I love my uncle as much as one can love another human." She paused. Her look became more serious. "He was the eldest son, in a business that gets passed from generation to generation. If he had had a choice, he'd have been a professor of art or history. But he had no choice."

She stopped for a moment, perhaps deciding what to reveal, then continued. "Recently I discovered that people have involved him in an insurance scheme, which I am trying to understand, in which people are dying."

I had to ask, "Is he the financial backer for people buying these insurance policies?"

She squeezed my hand. "I believe only as an investor. My uncle has become very ill. He's not been able to pay attention as he should. People are taking advantage of his illness and doing things he would never condone. I must find out what they are doing and protect my fami..." she stopped and corrected herself , "Uncle Vitorio's reputation."

A tear had formed in the corner of her eye. She turned away for a moment, clearly not wanting me to see, and then turned back. "You are the only person I can trust, who is capable of helping."

In watching her review the photos of her family, I understood. Now that they had all passed, she alone was responsible for her family's place in history.

Instinctively I felt affection, compassion. I put my arm around her and pulled her close, as one would a little girl who had fallen and scratched her knee. She relaxed into me, as though assuming the role I had created for her, then she tensed and pulled back. For a moment she looked away, seemingly embarrassed by her momentary show of vulnerability. Finally she faced me again, her head bowed slightly. "I am sorry, Anthony, my family has been the center of my life, and you are correct, they are all gone."

She lifted her head and at the same time I leaned toward her. We looked at each other, only inches apart for what seemed like an endless few seconds. In an instant my feelings of caring for the tearful little girl were replaced by an arousal of desire. She too must have felt the change. I could see the tension leave her body. She smiled, then her soft lips closed and moved quickly to mine. I kissed her back, gently at first, tasting the salt from her hidden tears.

My mind slowly emptied, no thoughts of past or future, I only knew the simple passion of my body for hers. My hand was on her neck softly stroking her hair. Her breathing became deeper as she pressed her body tightly against mine. Her kisses took on a passion which was more than a match for my own.

Ever since that first smile, the light touch of her fingers brushing my back, the whispered "good night," the last few days had contained a kaleidoscope of fantasies streaming endlessly and growing more erotic with each encounter. I was fighting to hold back an overwhelming desire to allow my hands to explore. Not wanting to move too quickly, I held her close, and waited, letting her determine the pace of what appeared inevitable.

Suddenly she pulled away. "I can't do this. It can only end in hurt, for us both." Her emotion had created a thicker accent than her normally perfect English.

Feeling like the recipient of a gift that, just as I was about to unwrap it, was suddenly wrenched away, I struggled for some magic words to regain what I had just lost.

Then I had a thought. If my feelings for her were only lust, I had lost the game. If it were not a game, if I were looking for more, hadn't I found it? Asking for my help, sharing her family history, and allowing me to see and feel her love for her family meant her feelings for me were much more than just sexual. I couldn't say I didn't feel lust, I did, but I also felt something else. Something much more, maybe more permanent, I wondered if she did, too.

With her hands, now resting at her sides, she quickly pushed herself from the couch and stood facing me. Again, I saw that sadness in her eyes that seemed internal, not related to me but to the circumstances of her life.

I stepped toward her, and took her gently in my arms. She rested her head on my chest. We stood quietly for a moment, then, almost in whisper, she said, "I'm sorry, Anthony. Thank you for being so understanding. There are things in my life I can't divulge. One day, if we remain close, you will find out, but not now."

She lifted her face from my chest to look directly at me. "I know you have seen me and felt a desire, perhaps a connection of some sort. What you don't know is that I have felt the same. After that first night, I asked several people about you, including Mrs. Fisher, who said she would arrange for us to meet."

Her smile had returned and brought a slight playfulness to her tone. Again I began thinking of what had almost been.

She continued, "After you paid her a visit, she called me. She said that although you tried not to be obvious, she could sense that the reason you came to visit was to ask her about me. She validated and encouraged my attraction to you. What doubts I may have had about getting involved with you, she put to rest." Gabriella stopped for a breath and moved closer.

I was trying to focus on what she was saying, while holding back those lusty desires lurking just beneath the surface. "Good old Mrs. Fisher, playing Cupid. I'll have to call and thank her."

She poked my chest with her finger, "Don't you dare. I told you this in confidence. The issue is this, Anthony. You should know by now, I am very attracted to you, and would love to have continued what we just started."

My mind was no longer a blank; this time the visions of her soft body were coming at warp speed.

"But anything we might have can only be temporary." She was still talking. I only heard, "and would have loved to continue what we started …" beyond that, I was barely picking up every third word.

"If we got involved it could not last."

I nodded, but neither understood nor cared about some vague future.

"Please. You must understand that."

I nodded, then again pulled her close. Our passion immediately reached the fevered pitch of only minutes before, but this time my hands began to explore.

She stopped me, this time for a different reason. Taking my hand she led me up a narrow stairway to her room and a king size bed. She pulled back the violet comforter to reveal the soft satin sheets, and turned to face me.

She held a hand to stop me. She stared into my eyes. "You understand?"

I nodded, and stepped toward her, this time her arms surrounded me pulling me close as she fell backward onto the bed.

The room was dark, but for the bright moon shining through the skylight.

Her voice was only a soft whisper between kisses. "Slow Anthony, slow. Our love can't last, give me memories."

I wasn't listening, nor paying attention to her words.

I should have.

# Chapter 25

In my dream I was running from someone, something. Then I was on a beach and a woman was rubbing oil onto my chest.

I woke to find Gabriella kneeling over me on the bed, tracing circles on my chest. The morning light was revealing the fullness of her body. I kissed her forehead. "Good morning, what are you doing?"

"I'm writing my name on your chest, to claim you."

As I pulled her close, I was suddenly struck by the reality of what my actions were committing me to. She had asked for my help; now I had to deliver. I had come to this sunny place to help Frank. He was at risk, possibly from the very person that Gabriella wanted me to help.

It would be normal for her to be blind to her uncle's bad deeds. What if he really was having people killed? Was it possible that by helping Gabriella I might increase the risk to Frank? One thing seemed clear; Tim Ryan was more dangerous than I had first thought. If Gabriella was right, Ryan could be a threat to both Vitorio and Frank, but in very different ways; to Vitorio's reputation, but to Frank's life.

I put my face next to hers and whispered softly in her ear, "I will do my best to help you, but you must understand, maybe nothing can be done. If your uncle is involved in this there is little I can do to help him."

She pulled away and faced me. "I know my uncle. Killing people for money is against his code. It is not his nature."

I thought about Mimi's read, "If he's involved in a scheme, it's much more complex than killing for money."

I decided to tell her about Frank's policy. Without mentioning the list, I told her a man named Tim Ryan had sold it to him.

"Yes, this Tim Ryan. I don't like him."

"Why?"

"I think he's the one who got my uncle involved."

"How do you know?"

She smiled. "My uncle is a quintessential Italian male. He would never discuss his business with me. But, when I first visited him in Boca two years ago, this man Ryan came to see him. Then he called several more times while I was there.

I listened. This is how I know it is about insurance. Six months ago Tim Ryan came again while I was there visiting. This time they argued. Uncle was very upset."

The fact that Gabriella had known Ryan was involved all along and never mentioned him made me wonder. I said to her, "Maybe you could ask George? I suspect George is somehow involved in all this."

"I don't see how my uncle could be involved in business dealings with George. Vitorio is an extremely intelligent and, as you might imagine, cautious man. Poor George is neither."

I didn't want to bring up the stolen list. It appeared there was a lot Gabriella wasn't telling me. I wasn't about to show her my full hand.

I continued, "Maybe Ryan got him involved. Maybe he has something on poor George. Gambling debts? It could be a lot of things."

I knew it was juvenile, but I really enjoyed saying "poor George."

"I don't think George even knows Tim Ryan."

She rolled closer to me and my thoughts turned to more pleasant pursuits.

Then I realized she was only reaching across me for the phone. She dialed a number.

"Hello George, would you take a starving woman to lunch?"

"B. and T.? Twelve thirty? Sounds good. No, I'll meet you there."

She put the phone down. "I'll do a little detective work of my own." She started to slide back across me.

No way was she was going to make it back to her side of the bed. There were still four hours until she had to meet George for lunch.

# Chapter 26

It was eleven, but the midday traffic was rush-hour slow. We'd spent the morning getting better acquainted than I thought possible and made plans to meet again that night.

She had to push me out the door, so she could get ready to meet George, a new experience for a guy who had once been a member of "The Morning After the Night Before Coyote Club."

Interspersed between bouts of passion, I had told her about the list I'd "stumbled onto," and anything else I could think of about Frank's case. In exchange she explained how she and George had met. Her uncle, wanting her to move into Palm Beach society at the proper level, had arranged it.

I didn't sense she was lying, but other than this one tidbit, I never got more than a superficial answer on anything. It wasn't exactly an equal trade.

Her objective was clear: extract Uncle Vitorio from the scam.

Mine was a little more complex. In order to protect Frank, and myself, I needed to determine how George, Tim Ryan, the Gibraltar Life, and the list were connected. Gabriella was confident Vitorio had only put up the money. She was blaming everything on Ryan. But I wasn't so sure. Vitorio had to be aware of the computer list that Ryan had been using for over three years.

Gabriella had been confident she could extract whatever we needed from George. After spending the last twelve hours with her, I didn't doubt that a bit. She said she had a plan. I told her I hoped it didn't include the techniques she had used on me. She gave me a kiss on the cheek, and smiled.

I picked up my cell and called Frank. I told him I had met with Gabriella, and that Vitorio was her adoptive uncle. There was a long silence, then a whistle.

I finished by saying she was going to meet George for lunch to try and determine his relationship to Tim Ryan."

"That's all very interesting, Tony. Where are you?" His tone had become more playful.

"I'm in my car."

"Where in your car?"

"Lantana."

"You wouldn't be just returning from Delray?"

"We can discuss that later. Your policy is with Gibraltar Life. Their home office is in Chicago. Is Tim Ryan from Chicago?"

"Yes. He was a broker with them, technically still is. But now he's focused on selling this package."

"Frank, Ryan started as a broker for Gibraltar Life in Chicago and Pagano's from Chicago. This can't be a coincidence."

I thought a minute then asked, "Were all the policies Ryan sold with Gibraltar?"

"I can't say all, but those I'm familiar with, yes."

Frank fell silent. I should have known the philosophy was coming.

"So, Tony. This Gabriella, love or lust? No, let me guess, when men are in love they talk constantly about the woman while omitting the romantic details. When they're in lust you get just the details. I'm getting nothing. You're in love."

"Thanks for defining that for me Frank. Let's get together and check the list against people you think were insured with Gibraltar. Meet me at the Marriott, say, two o'clock?"

"Tony, remember what Oscar Wilde said, 'A man can be happy with any woman, as long as he doesn't love her'."

"Bye, Frank."

As I drove, I wondered if Gabriella was using sex to manipulate me. Making love on our first meeting alone didn't seem to fit a woman with her traditional background and family values.

# Chapter 27

First thing back in the room, I called my former partner Brian. "Bri. Ever do any business with Gibraltar Life?"

"Sure, a few substandard cases. They're pretty competitive with health problems at the older ages."

"What percentage of people over eighty would you say were rated a higher premium or got rejected altogether?"

"What crazy crime are you investigating now, Tony?"

"Companies selling and financing policies for resale."

"We don't touch that stuff. Seems contrary to what insurance is all about. I think they'll kill it. No pun intended. To answer your question, my six partners at ABG and I don't have a large enough number of sales in that age to say for sure, but I'd guess at least fifty to sixty percent get rejected or charged extra. Most of our brokerage goes through Miles or Gary. They do primarily substandard stuff, so they'd have a better idea. I'll check with them and call you back. What's this all about?"

"Thanks Bri. When I figure it out, I'll tell you."

Something was out of whack. I just couldn't put my finger on it.

My cell had a couple of messages: Kate, checking to see if I was OK; a call from Sonja, "Please call, I have info on George." The third was from a number I didn't recognize. "Mr. T, Zack at the Brazilian, call me right away." That's the kid that valets my car. The message was from last night. I dialed the number.

"Hello." He sounded half asleep.

"Zack, Mr. T. What's up, buddy? Did I wake you?"

"No sir, I'm just here with a friend enjoying my day off." Memories of my earlier morning with "a friend" came flowing back. "I thought you'd be interested to know. A fellow came by last night. He was asking about you."

"What did you tell him?"

"Guy was a real tipper, gave me a big five bucks. I told him I didn't remember whether I'd seen you yesterday or not. I'm not always at the door and sometimes you don't take your car. You like to walk. He didn't think to ask if your car was there, and I didn't volunteer. He may have asked at the front desk. I doubt he got anywhere, they're very careful about revealing anything about their guests."

"What did the guy look like?"

"Short, stocky, black crew cut. You know him?"

"What was he driving?"

"Didn't see. Sorry."

"Thanks, Zack. If he comes back, I took a cab to the airport, went to Boston for a few days. Maybe you'll get another five out of him."

I could tell he was chuckling to himself. "Sounds good, Mr. T; if he comes back, I'll keep you posted."

"Thanks, Zack. I owe you."

"No problem."

He hung up, probably wanted to get back to his friend.

So, Ryan was trying to track me down, hopefully not for Mr. Pagano.

I visualized Gabriella begging for my life, Uncle Vitorio holding me by the throat and suggesting I leave Palm Beach and never see her again.

I called Sonja. She had her usual upbeat voice. "Hi baby, I tried to reach you last night. No return until now? You get lucky?"

Sonja has always wanted me to meet a nice girl and settle down, but the feeling that Gabriella's primary motivation was Vitorio's reputation, and that I was somewhere down her list, made me hesitate. I replied, "As Frank would say, that's all I've got is luck, no skill involved. Unfortunately, no. I guess my phone didn't pick it up until today."

"Guess what Tony? George has had gambling debts, big ones, and this guy Tim Ryan has ties to bookmakers. He plays a lot of golf with guys from Jupiter that take book."

"Well, Sergeant, they certainly promoted the right person. I hope you aren't wasting your time on my case, instead of working on police business."

Now that I was involved with Gabriella, I realized dividing my loyalties between them would be a problem.

"Believe me, if what you think is happening really is, this could get me promoted to Lieutenant."

But backing off was not Sonja's strong suit. I could picture her marching Vitorio off in handcuffs, and Gabriella begging me to free him. It wasn't a pleasant image. I needed time to think. "If I pick up any more information, I'll let you know."

"And Tony, one more thing. Absolutely keep this to yourself. You know the barges that pump sand from the channel to restore the beach? Guess what was coming out of the pipes?"

"I don't know, what?"

"Body parts! We don't know whether someone fell off a tanker and was sucked into the pipes, or someone was chopped up and thrown in with the sand. We have a part of an arm and a leg. The lab is checking for rope marks or bruises. We need to keep it real quiet until we get more details. The press will go crazy. It's not exactly great publicity for Palm Beach's tourist trade."

"Insurance companies take years to pay on missing persons."

I realized I was now trying to defend Uncle Vitorio. It was weird how quickly my allegiance had shifted.

"You never know, Tony. Seems like the sort of thing the Mafia would do to send a message."

I put down the phone and lay back on the bed, rubbing my temples. I had, as the girls say, "Too much information."

I must have dozed off, the phone was ringing. Frank was on his way up.

# Chapter 28

He gave me his usual wide grin and hug, put a hand on each shoulder and looked me straight in the eye. "Tony I just want you to know how much I appreciate your infiltrating the enemy camp to protect me."

Now the grin was gone. "You're a bright guy Tony, but never forget. The brightest guy in the country is putty in the hands of a smart, good-looking woman. I've met this Gabriella. She's more than just smart, and her uncle comes first. Be careful, for both of us. OK?"

I wanted to protest, explain how she was different. Before I could get a word out, Frank put his index finger to his lips. "Nuff said, let's get to the list."

We checked through the obituaries for the three names Frank had given to Tim Ryan.

Jack Taylor, age 86, cancer.

Mario Dennis, age 82, long illness.

Nathan Lord, age 81, heart failure.

We sat staring at each other.

"What do you think, Frank? How can they be killing people with heart failure and cancer?"

Frank stood and stretched, then walked to the window. He was quiet for a full two minutes, then turned back and smiled. "What if they're insuring people that already have heart problems and cancer? What if they all had the same doctor and he's improving their records before they get sent out?"

"Stranger things have happened. Particularly down here." I replied.

"We probably can determine who their doctor was. Palm Beach has its own walk in clinic. I'll bet all these people are members. Their records would show who their primary physician was," said Frank.

I know what you're thinking, Frank. The answer is no!"

"Relax, you don't need to do anything illegal. I know a woman who works there. I helped her son out of a jam. I bet she'd take a quick peek at the files to see if they had the same doc. I'll take her to lunch and ask. No problem."

While Frank was talking, I was looking on the computer for James Maguire's accident report. Driving alone, late afternoon on South County, ran into a tree. Skid marks revealed he might have swerved to avoid a car coming in the opposite direction. If he had, the other car hadn't stopped. I pointed to the screen.

"This definitely looks like he could have been done in for the insurance."

"Didn't you make plans to see Jennifer Maguire for golf at Everglades? The family may have suspicions about what happened." He gave me a pat on the cheek. "I'll bet a charmer like you can get it out of her."

"Good idea, Frankie. I'll call her right now and confirm that invitation. Find out about the doctor from your friend at the clinic, and we'll talk later."

I had a stack of cards in my desk; Jennifer's was near the top. I picked up the phone as Frank was letting himself out.

"Hello, Jennifer? This is Anthony Tauck. We met at your dad's funeral."

I realized how strange that sounded. She seemed OK with it.

"Why yes, Mr. Tauck, I do remember. You're the fellow who thought my father was patient, and that I was an old lady. Weren't we going to play golf?"

"That's not exactly a fair interpretation of what I said, but why don't we settle it on the golf course."

"I planned to play in the morning. Would you be available then?"

"Absolutely, what time?"

"I have a 9:15. If you'd like to practice, come early."

"Sounds great, see you there." I hung up and read the obit again. It hadn't changed.

# Chapter 29

"Anthony. I have a nice surprise for you."

I loved her voice. It brought back some thoughts that ought to be censured.

"You are a nice surprise for me."

"No, seriously, you may want to hire me as an assistant when you find what I have gotten from George."

"What? What did you find?"

"Give me directions to where you are staying. I'll come to your place at six."

I gave her the directions, but wondered if I should have. Much as I was anxious to see her, I saw the validity in Frank's concern. Her uncle came first. She had evaded most of my questions, and had only volunteered that she knew about Tim Ryan after I brought him up.

Other parts of her history didn't fit right.

Her mother was Giacometti's daughter, yet she's a Giacometti.

Uncle Vitorio was always in the picture. Did her father work for him? Maybe this whole Giacometti story was a cover. Maybe Ryan works for Pagano and always had.

I called her back. "Gabriella, when you get to the Marriott, leave your car with the doorman. Walk through the lobby. Go to the right, there's a small coffee shop in the rear of the building. I'll meet you there."

"What is this all about, Anthony?"

"You have a secret, I have a secret. Meet me there at six."

"Of course," she sighed, and hung up.

It was after five. I didn't have much time. I called for my car, and headed down on the elevator. It was waiting at the front door. I gave the valet a five, and drove my car out to the main street going east. I took a left at the first light, then another left until I had circled around to the alley behind the Marriott. The area was a little seedy. I locked the car, and banged on the door to the service entrance. A handsome young man, probably Cuban, opened the door and smiled. I thanked him as I brushed by and headed back to my room.

My small balcony faced the street. I slid open the glass door and waited. It wasn't long before Gabriella's little gray Toyota pulled into the driveway. I didn't want her to have to wait, but I had to delay a minute. Sure enough, the same green BMW I had seen that night at Kate's pulled up and parked across the street. It had to be Ryan. My phone was ringing. I let it ring and headed to the elevator. I wondered, had she led them or did they follow?

I was lucky. People were getting off on my floor. After what seemed like forever, I was on the ground floor heading out back to the coffee shop.

She had her back to me, wearing a sleeveless green jersey and tight white pants. I grabbed her arm and whispered "Someone's following you." I hurried her through the service exit to my car.

Trotting to keep up, Gabriella said, "Anthony, what's this about? Where are we going? What do you mean someone is following me? Who?"

I opened the passenger door, helped her in, jumped in and drove. I knew they'd come looking. I needed to get out of the area before they realized we were gone.

"Gabriella, did you call my room?"

"No! What's this all about?"

We were heading west on Okeechobee. I needed to get to Interstate 95 without being spotted. It must have been Ryan that called, I thought. When I didn't answer, they must have picked up on what we were doing.

I reached over and took her hand. "Sorry to rush you out like that. Tim Ryan was parked across the street from the hotel. He must have followed you. Does he know your car?"

"I don't think so, but I hadn't thought to hide where I was going."

"He and another man have been checking on me, looking for me. I'm staying at Brazilian Court. To avoid them I rented another car and moved to the Marriott."

She turned to face me. "What have I done?"

She leaned over and put her head against my shoulder and her hand on my thigh. "I'm so sorry. I must have led them to you. But how would they know I was meeting you?"

When she touched me, my desire was back. It was nearly impossible to think clearly. Frank was right. I was putty, and she hadn't even started talking. Underestimating her could be hazardous. Somehow I didn't care.

I snuggled my arm around her shoulder and drove slowly for another ten minutes, keeping an eye on the mirror for the 750. No sign of it, so at PGA I turned east and traveled a couple of blocks to the parking lot at Carmine's. I pulled around the back, where I hoped we wouldn't be seen. All the while I was wondering if her concern was real. I was driving myself crazy with the second guessing. I had to confront her.

I turned off the engine and pulled her close. "Gabriella, this situation is getting dangerous. You must tell me the truth. Did your uncle get you together with George only for the social contacts?"

She smiled. She enjoyed talking positively about her uncle. "My uncle is a very sophisticated man. He's been coming to Palm Beach for years and has many legitimate friends and business associates. He had a friend at George's firm introduce us. He wanted me to meet the better people in Palm Beach society. He said it would happen through George. He was right." She paused and smiled. "My uncle is, as they say, playing chess when others are playing checkers. Of course he had other motives, but he legitimately wanted what was best for me."

I had to push her on the lies. "You knew George and Tim Ryan were acquainted, didn't you?"

She dropped her chin, looked down at the seat, and then looked straight at me. "Yes, I was with George when he got calls from Ryan. I was afraid to tell you. I thought you would assume my uncle was involved and wouldn't trust me, wouldn't help me."

"Do you think George is involved with Tim Ryan in this insurance deal?"

She probably sensed from my tone that I was trying to believe her, but wasn't quite able to.

She reached into her purse, pulled out her cell phone, and handed it to me.

I turned it on. A number came on the face that I didn't recognize. "This isn't your number. Is this your phone?"

She gave me a smile that was a cross between Dorothy in the Wizard of Oz, and Mata Hari. "No. It's George's phone, he has mine."

She pulled a second phone from her purse identical to the first. "By the time he realizes we switched phones, we'll have all his numbers. When his phone rings, this new one will ring too."

"Do both phones have the same programmed number?"

"Yes, I have a friend in the mobile phone store. I brought in George's phone and he copied the chip. You wanted to know if he and Ryan are acquainted. Three of his last ten calls were from Tim Ryan."

"Have you listened?"

"There's a message that Ryan left last night."

She pushed the button and held it to my ear.

"George, give me a call. Sidney needs a payment. Oh, by the way, do you know a guy by the name of Tauck? We think he may be the one who stole the list. We traced the car seen leaving my parking lot Sunday morning. The cleaning guy said it was a silver 600 SL. It had to be him. He's staying at the Brazilian."

Clearly it was Ryan. I handed the phone back. "What's this 'Sidney needs a payment?' Who's Sidney?"

"That's George's bookmaker. George loves to gamble. I guess it makes him feel like a man. I fear he only tells me when he wins. I really am fond of George. He lives in such a shadow of his father. Nothing he does is ever good enough." She was quiet for a moment.

"Oh! I didn't tell you. When we met for lunch I asked George about his involvement with Tim Ryan. He seemed taken aback by the question, but said his firm had to approve and oversee all insurance purchases. George was put in charge of that area about four years ago. Then I told him about Tim Ryan's meeting with my uncle two years ago, and that they had met recently."

I was going to press her on whether she believed George's connection to Ryan was more than firm business, but her phone started to ring. She held it in her palm like a living thing. We both stared and waited.

Finally, she pressed the message key and held the phone away from her ear so I could listen. It wasn't good.

"George, call me. I followed your girlfriend to the Marriott at City Place. She went in an hour ago and hasn't come out. On a hunch, I called and asked for Tauck's room, no answer. He's registered at the Marriott and the Brazilian. Something's not right."

Gabriella put down the phone. For a moment we just stared at each other. I could tell she felt guilty. She had led Ryan directly to me. I gave her a hug. "Not your fault. Maybe George was suspicious of the questions you were asking and called Ryan. Did he get up at all during the lunch?"

"Yes, but he didn't take his cell. That's when I switched phones. I'd been teasing him, said his phone was better-looking than mine."

"They know I have the list and computer disks. A lot of people on both sides would like them back."

She gave me a puzzled look. "What do you mean, both sides?"

"Ryan wants the list because if people on it are dying it's pretty incriminating, plus it contains some very private information that powerful people would not want public."

"Why don't we give the list back? Negotiate a truce?"

"I think it's too late. Ryan and whoever he's involved with are by now as concerned that we may have figured out what he's doing with the list, as getting it back."

"I see. The list is evidence. It connects the people who died and probably has Tim Ryan's fingerprints all over it."

"Yah, and mine. At this point the list is of more value confirming that some scheme exists. I'm the other evidence, and unlike the list, I can talk."

She suddenly looked worried. "You think they want to kill you?"

"I don't know if they would go that far, but no sense finding out."

I paused and thought a minute, then continued. "By now they must know Frank and I are friends and why I'm involved. This phone may help to prove your uncle isn't involved."

I watched her to see how she reacted to my statement. She had been trying to keep up the front that her uncle was only involved as an investor, but a few new furrows across her normally smooth forehead suggested that she was no longer sure.

I headed back to I-95 and turned north, away from Palm Beach. It had gotten dark. She leaned against me. "Where are we going?"

"They'll be looking for us. Let's find a place to spend the night."

She leaned closer and put her hand on my shoulder. "I feel safe with you, Anthony."

Great, I only wished I felt safe with me.

# Chapter 30

The room was pitch black, only the slit between the curtains on the sliding glass door allowed in any light. I rolled slowly onto my side and sat up on the edge of the bed, trying not to wake Gabriella.

I could see the digital clock, 5:45. I picked up my pants from the floor, where I'd kicked them off in a hurry. As my eyes adjusted to the light, I saw the cell phone beside the bed, I picked it up, and quietly stepped out into the motel hallway. I dressed in the hall and headed to the lobby. I could smell coffee brewing.

My old partner, Brian, would be in the office by six. I needed to know if he had any information on Gibraltar Life. Frank would have found out from his friend at the clinic if the so-called victims had the same doctor. It didn't seem likely, but nothing else about this case seemed likely either.

While sipping my coffee, I checked George's phone. We hadn't turned it off. I was hoping to listen in if Tim called. There were two messages from late last night. We would have been too "busy" to have heard it ring.

"George, you need to get in touch. Where are you? I've got problems. And if I got problems, you got problems." The second was similar.

Finally it dawned on me, Gabriella had George's phone as well as the duplicate. George was only getting Gabriella's messages not his own. Unless Ryan had seen George in person, George didn't know that Gabriella had come to the Marriott, let alone run off with me.

Gabriella needed to get to George before Tim did. I ran back to the room and sat beside her on the bed, "Honey, wake up." I grasped her bare shoulder, shaking her gently. She sat up slowly, rubbing her eyes. She reached for me and the sheet slipped to her waist revealing her flat stomach, the curve of her hips and a lot more.

No sense waking George too early. I pulled her down beside me.

She was lying with her head on my shoulder, her arm draped across my waist. She had been telling me something about her childhood, and like a typical guy after sex, I was only half listening. My phone rang. I picked it up slowly, not wanting to cause her to move away. It was Brian.

"Tony, I got something that might help. I told Gary what you were looking for. He said, 'Have Tony call me about my pal Dino. He's my goomba from Chicago in Gibraltar's underwriting department. Gary thinks you may have hit on something. If this guy Ryan isn't getting rejections on eighty-year-olds, he's got an inside track to someone. If it's not Dino, Dino will probably know who it is."

"Thanks again, Bri, I'll talk to you later."

I passed the phone to Gabriella. "You need to get to George before Ryan does. He's not getting Ryan's messages. It's close to seven. I need to drop you at your car, get changed, and get to the Everglades by 8:30. Hopefully, they'll have given up on waiting for us at the Marriott."

She took the phone, sat up against the headboard, and dialed a number. "George's private line, Tim Ryan wouldn't have it." She held her index finger to her lips. "George, I feel so foolish. I have your phone. Do you have mine? Good. Is there any way you can bring it to Delray? I'll cook you a nice brunch."

There was a pause. "You are so sweet, my place at ten? See you then."

She gave me a long sad stare. "I hope George isn't too involved in this. He's really sweet and has been so caring to me."

I rolled off the bed. "Let's get moving. We haven't got much time."

# Chapter 31

Some of my friends think every day is a great day for golf. When I was a new golfer and still had illusions that I could play, so did I. Improvements came sporadically, but it wasn't my sport. Now I enjoy the social aspect. Expecting little from my game, I enjoy it more.

I drove into the circle, where a valet took my car. I was greeted by a very proper older woman with a British accent. "You must be Mr. Talk. Please let me take you to Miss Maguire on the pavilion."

I decided correcting the pronunciation of my name might spoil her performance; I let it go.

We passed through a heavy glass door into an open area with white wicker furniture. Ficus trees provided shade for the morning breakfasters.

Jennifer was on the putting green. My clubs had been placed on her cart nearby.

She shook my hand, and leaned forward so I might kiss her cheek.

"I'm so glad you called. I thought about my father having the patience with you that he never had with me. Maybe you're more relaxed, more casual about your game, than I."

I was feeling uncomfortable with my little white lie about playing with her father.

"A quick pointer for someone he'd never see again versus a daughter he was very proud of. Let me guess. Of all your siblings, you're most like your father."

She gave me a curious look, nodded and said softly, "I was very close to my dad."

I needed to get off the subject of her father before I got myself into a corner. "Are you warmed up? I don't play that often. I'd need hours to get my game in shape."

She hopped into the cart. I drove.

It didn't take long for Jennifer's competitive side to disappear. On the second hole, I sculled a ball out of the trap, into the woods, and laughed. After that our game got social.

On the third tee she said, "I guess you've played here before. You seem to know the distances without looking at the card."

I told her I played here many times in years past, and who I was married to. She said, "Anthony, if you lasted ten years with that woman looking over your shoulder, you can get along with anyone." I was happy that she shared my opinion of my mother-in-law. I had a soul mate, with great legs to boot.

The round became a conversation interspersed by golf shots. Jennifer seemed pretty grounded for having grown up in the Palm Beach social whirl. I finally asked my question: "What was your dad like?"

She laughed. "He grew up with wealth, but was ambitious, believed in hard work for himself and his four children. I made two dollars an hour working at McDonald's while my friends drove hot cars and partied. My siblings and I turned out well, in spite of too much money. I can't say that for a lot of my friends. My dad worked hard past age seventy, then had to retire. 'A bad ticker' was how he described it."

My ears perked up. "Strange he should survive a bad heart to die in an accident."

"We think, that is Bill Bradley thinks, that a heart attack may have caused the accident. That's not for publication, by the way."

"Guess it doesn't matter at this point does it? Bill Bradley, is he the physician most Palm Beach families use?"

"Yes. He's a member here. He comes from a fine family, is an excellent physician and very discrete, a not unimportant trait in this town."

We had finished our game, I felt good about my 89. The course is short so I never took out my driver. No holes with a ball in the woods makes a big difference in your score. Next to her 78, mine was no great shakes.

The day had gotten hot, even in the shade, so we took a table inside for lunch. My curiosity was getting the best of me. Finally I asked, "Tell me if it's none of my business, but you're still a Maguire. You never married?"

She laughed, kind of a low chuckle. "Of course I've been married, in fact twice. I don't seem to make very good choices. I always fall for the wrong type, and there's always the money issue."

"What's the money issue?"

"If you have it, you never know whether they're after you, or the money."

"That's kind of sad. You obviously have a lot more going for you than money."

She gave me a flirty smile, batted her eyes, and gave me her best Blanche DuBois imitation. "Why Mr. Tauck, I do declare, you say the sweetest things."

She was an appealing woman, but a lot had happened since the night at the funeral home, not the least of which was the last two nights spent with Gabriella. I wasn't sure if she thought I was interested and was giving me an opening, or what. I knew I needed to get out of there.

Thank God for watches. You can always check your watch, seem surprised the time has flown and say you're late for a meeting. That's exactly what I did. I felt a little guilty, but rationalized, it was for Frank.

As soon as I got to my car, I checked my cell. Nothing from Gabriella, one from Kate. I called Frank. We planned to meet at Starbucks on Clematis.

# Chapter 32

I cut down Coconut Row past the Flagler Museum. While still married to his second wife, who was institutionalized, Henry Flagler, the man who created Florida as we know it today, got the legislature to declare insanity grounds for divorce so he could marry his third wife, Mary Lily. The museum is a fifty-five room home built for her in 1902 as a wedding gift. I don't know if that law is still in effect, but suspect more than one Palm Beacher, male and female, has wished they could use it.

As I crossed the northern bridge, I returned Kate's call. She picked up right away. "Tony, guess what? You're going to promote me to junior detective."

I had to smile. She'd often kidded me about having a better ability to read people than I did. She was probably right. "OK, you're promoted. What's the scoop?"

As I listened, I took a left off Dixie onto Clematis. Usually I have to park and walk a few blocks. I lucked out, there was a space directly in front of Starbucks. I turned off the ignition as she continued.

"I had dinner with my friend Jeannie Carlson. She's the receptionist at Bingham, Burroughs, DuPont I was telling you about. I said you were visiting and about this guy Ryan being in the street in front of the house. By the way, Jeannie's very pretty. Slim with a huge chest. Not your type." She laughed.

I kept still. I knew anything I said both could and would be used against me.

Then Kate's voice went up about three decibels. "Tony, she's seen this guy Ryan with George Bingham. What's that about?"

"Ryan sells insurance to firm clients, and George approves it. Strictly business."

"Not so, Anthony. Jeannie said these two have more than a business relationship. They talk all the time. She thinks they own a business together.

Kate had confirmed what I already surmised, but I didn't want to discourage her. "Wow! You are promoted. That fills in a big piece of the puzzle. But look, I'm meeting Frank. Can I call you later?"

"Sure honey, be careful."

Good old Kate. There are networks of people who run offices, sell real estate, and work in the restaurants. They know everything that's happening; she's a member of all three. I'll bet she could have told me things about Gabriella and Vitorio, but I wasn't asking. I really didn't want to put her at risk.

Inside, I got a surprise. Frank was sitting against the wall, Sonja was facing him. What was she doing here? Frank knows a lot of things about Gabriella and Vitorio that I hadn't gotten into with Sonja, and wasn't sure I wanted to, at least not yet. She turned and waved. "Tony! Over here."

I gave her a kiss on the cheek. Frank patted the seat next to him. I sat, not sure what we were discussing. I looked over at Sonja.

Frank slapped the table in front of me. "So what happened with Jennifer?"

"She shot a 78. I shot an 89."

"OK smart guy. Did you get her to talk about her father's accident? That's why Sonja's here."

I was relieved. Frank knew what I was thinking and wanted to put me at ease.

"Was the accident an accident? They're not certain it was. She told me on the QT he had a bad heart. Their doctor, Bill Bradley, examined the body and felt Jim possibly had a heart attack which caused the accident."

Sonja spoke up. "The family wants it to appear like an accident to collect more? That doesn't sound like something they would do."

Frank and I said almost in unison. "No accidental death after seventy."

"So it doesn't matter," she said. "They just want to let it be.

Sonja stood up. "Well, I've got to get back to solving crimes."

She reached across and gave Frank's hand a pat.

I stood to say goodbye, then moved to her chair to face Frank. "What did you find out at the clinic?

Frank looked at me and wrinkled his forehead. "It looks like several of the names on the list had the same doctor, this guy Bradley."

I said, "Is Palm Beach's favorite doc on the level?"

Frank was rubbing his stomach. "I'm starved, let's run next door to Rocco's. We can talk."

The restaurant is open to the street. We took a booth inside by the far wall. I didn't want Ryan or one of his pals to happen by and spot us by accident. (There's that bad word again.)

Frank ordered a small steak; I ordered a coffee and ate his bread. He leaned back, ran his fingers through his hair and finally said, "Hard to know if Doc Bradley's involved in Ryan's deal.

Any requests for medical records are handled by him personally. Usually that's a Xerox job for a clerk. It might be he's protective of patients who are friends, or he could be controlling all information that leaves his office."

I said, "Yah, easy to pull out a negative test from a file and make a person appear healthier than he is, particularly if the underwriter at Gibraltar is in on the deal."

Frank shrugged. "We need more background on Bradley. There are more than a few grandchildren in this town curious about the health of their meal ticket."

He hesitated and gave me that look. "So Tony, what's the story with Miss Milan?"

I never know what direction Frank is coming from. I led with my chin.

"Gabriella is definitely on our side." I thought that would get a rise, but he sat quietly and listened. I hadn't seen him this serious for some time. Attending Maguire's wake may have woken him up to thoughts of his own mortality.

I explained in detail how Gabriella had come to the Marriott, been followed by the BMW, and about our trip to PGA. Without thinking who I was with, I stopped and said, "I need another coffee."

Frank reached across and gave my cheek a pat. "Little sleepy, Tony? I want you to know how much I appreciate those long sleepless nights you're putting in on my behalf."

The waitress brought me another coffee.

Before he could start in again, I told him how Gabriella had swapped phones with George and then had a friend duplicate the chip. When I told him we picked up the messages from Ryan, he sat up straight. "Have you spoken to her? Did she swap back?"

I shook my head, pulled out my phone, and dialed her home number. It rang several times then stopped. It seemed like someone had picked it up, held it for a few seconds, then hung it up. I looked over at Frank.

Frank shook his head. "It's after three. She was going to meet George at ten. If she hasn't got her cell back by now, they're on to her."

My phone was ringing.

"Hi babe." It was Sonja. "I finally got some information on that BMW. I asked the computer guy at the station to flag the number and call me. He picked the license up when the car crossed the Southern Bridge. I was on Worth Avenue when he called. I caught up with them on A1A, heading south toward Delray. I told them they were speeding. It was Ryan and his driver, Freddie Spring. He's from Boca, a loose cannon, got a few assault charges, a little jail time. Spring could be an enforcer; I don't know his connection to Ryan."

"What do you mean enforcer?"

"Collects overdue loans, breaks a few heads."

"Like George's gambling debts?"

"Possible."

"Thanks. You're the best." I hung up and told Frank.

"Call her cell, Tony. She could be in big trouble."

This time, she picked up. "Hello, is that you Anthony?" Her voice sounded heavy, hesitant.

"Honey, I was worried."

"They came for George, Tony. I'm worried."

"Who came? Are you OK?"

"I am now. Ryan and another man came to the house. They must have followed George."

"Stay there. We'll be right down."

# Chapter 33

Frank drove. I dialed my brokerage friend. Gary's been around the block, knows how to schmooze and entertain underwriters at companies like Gibraltar. Reviewing medical records and setting a rate is not an exact science. More than one underwriter has done a favor and slipped one through.

"Gary, it's Tony Tauck. How are things in the desert?"

"You think I don't recognize that voice? How are you, buddy?"

"Life is good, but I need some help. Brian said you mentioned an underwriter with Gibraltar Life who likes to get people covered. Does a guy named Dino fit the bill?"

He laughed. "Dino's very cooperative. Course, I've been known to find him a little Arizona vacation time in midwinter. He's getting close to retirement, doing all his friends favors. You need something?"

"Yah, I need find out if he knows a guy named Ryan, Tim Ryan."

"No problem. Dino and I go back a long way. What's this about?"

I knew I could trust Gary, so I expanded on what Brian had probably told him.

Gary gave a loud whistle and promised to call back.

When we finally arrived at Gabriella's, she ran out her front door and threw her arms around my neck. "Oh Anthony, they took George. What will they do to him?"

Frank answered, "Just scare him. They need George to keep approving the sales."

Sounded good. I wondered if she believed it.

Once inside, I spotted what looked like pieces of a china dinner plate, under the table that held the linen samples. An accident?

I had to wonder, if Vitorio was as sick as Gabriella said, wouldn't she have gotten rid of the fabric?

I put my arm around Gabriella. "Are you alright?"

"Yes, I'm fine." She gave me a weak smile. I wasn't convinced.

"What did they do to you, Gabriella?"

"I'm OK. The man I didn't know was a little rough. Ryan called him Freddie. He was dark, a large, heavy man, very crude.

Ryan told him to stop."

Frank asked a logical question. "Do George and Ryan know Vitorio is your uncle?"

"I've known George for some time. He has been with me in Vitorio's company; he may suspect we are related, but I was introduced to George as Vitorio's art dealer and family friend. Tim Ryan doesn't know."

"What about the phone? Did you trade with George?"

"Yes. The copy of George's phone is there in the drawer."

Frank pulled it out and flicked it on. "This has Ryan's cell in the memory. Should we call him?"

"No. Wait," I said. "Maybe Gary will call back with some info about Dino. We can make Ryan think we know his game. There must have been several claims already paid with more to come. We could threaten to tip off the company."

I was beginning to doubt whether George had really been forced to leave the house. What if it was all a farce to make Gabriella think he was less involved than he was? The linen samples probably made them think Vitorio was still on the scene, may have given her some protection.

I picked up the phone and was flicking through the messages when it occurred to me that Ryan's phone voice sounded oddly familiar. I hand the phone to Frank, who was comforting Gabriella, "Listen to Ryan's voice on this message to George."

He looked at me like I was a little strange, then curiosity and his realization that Gabriella was upset, prompted him to press the keys to listen. He smiled. I knew he was be listening to Ryan's message about our escape from the Marriott. He held the phone another minute, pressed another button and wrote down a number. He shut the phone off and placed it on the table with the suit samples. "Tony, that's amazing."

Just then, my phone rang. It was Gary. "Hey buddy, I reached Dino. No luck, said he'd heard of Ryan, but couldn't recall doing business with him, at least not lately."

"Did he have any suggestions as to who might be handling his cases?"

"No, but he seemed in a hurry to get me off the phone. Not typical Dino, he's always got a story to tell."

"Thanks, Gar."

I turned to Frank who was still smiling. "Dino says he doesn't know Ryan, but Gary was suspicious by the way Dino rushed him off the phone."

Frank repeated his statement. "Tony, that's amazing."

With a smirk I concurred, "Yup, on the phone, Ryan sounds like you with a cold. Why don't you call Dino and say you're Ryan, but do it quick. If Dino's involved, he's probably already trying to reach Ryan."

Frank called the operator for the main number. "Operator, could you connect me with the underwriting department?"

He waited "Hello. Is there a secretary or an underwriter who sits near Dino?"

Frank had lowered his voice. He did sound surprisingly like Tim Ryan. I wondered what he was up to.

"Hello, Dino's line is busy. Could you patch me into his voice mail?" He waited a minute then continued. "Dino, my cell is out. Call me on George's phone 561-514-..." He gently placed the phone on the table, as though moving it abruptly would influence the result.

"Might as well take a chance with a bigger net."

Gabriella looked first at Frank then me. "You think George is involved in this?"

I hesitated. There was no reason I should feel jealous of George, but if I were the one to accuse, it might have that tone.

The phone on the table rang. No one moved. It rang again several times. I looked at Gabriella, then Frank, then at the phone. Finally, Frank picked it up. He held it so I could see the number on the face. 773-528-6090, Gibraltar Life. "We got a break, George's phone is off. Dino's leaving a message."

Another thirty seconds, the dial cleared. He punched the message button, put it on speaker, and set it on the table. We huddled close to listen.

"Timmy! One of my brokers is asking about you. Wants to know who underwrites your cases. The broker is originally from Boston. Isn't that guy Tauck from Boston? Someone is still in the guessing stage, but getting warmer. Call me back. What's with my calling George's phone? When we started this deal Vitorio said, 'Keep this between the two of us, with George on the fringe.' Sharing a phone ain't on 'the fringe,' and Doc Bradley's not 'the two of us'. Vitorio will not be happy if he finds we've involved George and Doc Bradley."

I was watching Gabriella's discomfort at hearing her uncle's name. There was something she wasn't telling us.

Frank spoke first. "Well, that answers the question about Doc Bradley. There've been rumors that his family's wealth has dwindled. His grandfather married twice and had four kids with each wife. Doc's living in the original family home. That trust income is being split up among too many people, and medicine doesn't pay like it used to. He may be struggling to keep the house. George's firm probably handles his family's investments. He would know if Bradley was in trouble."

I was listening but watching Gabriella. Frank and I were just now learning things she probably knew.

Finally she spoke. She sounded contrite, like she should have mentioned it earlier. "One night, after a meeting with Ryan, my uncle was visibly upset. I was concerned and confronted him, which is uncharacteristic of me. He explained that he had invested in an honest business deal with Ryan, but Ryan was doing things he didn't approve of, including using my uncle's name for leverage, which he really didn't like."

Gabriella was pacing back and forth, as though it helped her remember. "I told Vitorio how George bragged that he had money and planned to leave his father's firm. I asked him if George was involved. He said no."

I still wondered if she was protecting him. "You think your uncle didn't know that George knew Tim Ryan?"

She shook her head. "He seemed genuinely upset. Ryan had just said no one else was involved. When I started spending more time with George, I found they were acquainted but I didn't know if it had to do with the insurance."

I wondered what else she hadn't told me. Had she known about Bradley? Certainly George bragged about making money independent of his father. He must have said something about where this money was coming from. Maybe she knew about Dino before today. She'd denied knowing George was involved, when she had actually suspected it.

I said nothing. I'd ask her what she knew when we were alone.

Frank was more direct. "Gabriella. You said that Ryan and Freddie had taken George by force. That and a number of other things you've been telling us are not true. We need the truth, or you're on your own." He grabbed the phone and started for the door. "Tony, we're outta here."

Gabriella looked to me for support. I wanted to rescue her, but I couldn't go against Frank. Plus, he was right.

"Anthony, I care for you; I need your trust. I am so sorry. I lied to protect my uncle. I got close to George, went though his papers, got into his computer, and when I could, I listened in on his calls to Tim Ryan."

She paused for a breath. "When you called I was arguing with Ryan. I told him I knew they were getting policies issued on unhealthy people. I told him to find a way to keep Vitorio out of it, or I would tell him. That's when that thug he travels with started to get a little rough. Ryan and George made him stop."

Frank seemed amused. "So you knew about the computer list all along?"

"Yes. Ryan wanted to use it to blackmail people. My uncle said no."

Frank hesitated then asked. "When did you find out about that?"

Gabriella, for all her normal composure, looked embarrassed. She turned to face me. "Anthony, remember I told you that Ryan visited my uncle about six months ago and they argued. That's when Ryan wanted to use it to extort money. My uncle was furious."

I had told her I had a list that first morning we were together, but I didn't mention Ryan. She already knew. Why wouldn't she have been a little more cautious when she came to the Marriott and led them right to me? I didn't want to bring it up in front of Frank, he had never trusted her. If she wasn't lying, she sure was avoiding the truth. I turned to Frank, trying to defend her I said "She's been trying to protect her uncle."

I had never lied to Frank before but I was getting real close now.

He wasn't buying it. "So, should we call Sonja and clue her in? She could provide some protection."

He turned to face Gabriella. His tone had an edge of anger. "Since you have an understanding of this scam, how safe am I?"

"How much insurance do they have on you, Frank?"

"Four million."

"I think there are others with up to ten. That was the maximum; something about spreading the risk. Most of the deaths were natural causes. Only Maguire was an accident."

Her answer implied that she knew a lot more than I had thought. I didn't get why she was admitting to Frank what she had hidden from me.

"So, I'm small potatoes," said Frank. "We know the other deaths seemed to be natural, but in this town, natural isn't always natural. Right, Tony?"

I thought about Mrs. Fisher and nodded. "Now what do we do? With the town's most trusted doctor on the payroll, anything's possible. And the computer sheets? Do they even matter any more?"

Frank shook his head. "I can see Doc Bradley screening medical records for insurance companies, but I can't believe he's in on a wholesale plot to poison people."

Gabriella had moved to the couch where we'd first made love. She seemed uncomfortable with Frank's questions and wanted to get out of his direct line of vision before she spoke, "Wouldn't the insurance companies deny the claims? Don't they check when people die?"

I sat next to her before I answered. "No, after a policy has been in effect two years they seldom check. Plus these companies are so big and slow moving they may not notice for years. A company the size of Gibraltar may pay out seventy-five to a hundred million bucks a day in normal claims. An extra five million here, five million there could take a while to be noticed."

I sensed a hint of relief come over her, but wasn't sure if it was for Frank, Uncle Vitorio, or herself.

Frank interrupted my little reverie. "Where is your uncle now, Gabriella?"

"He's in Chicago. Why?"

"I'd like to meet him. Maybe we can settle this quietly."

She hesitated. "As I told you, he's been quite ill; let me figure how to approach him. There are a lot of things I now know that I haven't told him."

Or me, I thought.

Frank looked at his watch. "The clinic's open tonight. I'm going to get sick and go see Doc Bradley. Your car is on Clematis, I'll give you a ride to your car."

I started to get up. Gabriella grabbed my arm. "Stay with me, Anthony. I don't want to be here alone. I'll give you a ride, or you can take my car, return it later."

I felt the warmth of her arm and breast against my side. I tried not to make eye contact with Frank. "I'll stay with her. Call me after you see Bradley."

I could tell he was annoyed. He didn't trust her, and wanted to talk to me alone.

Of course I rationalized that Gabriella would tell me more when we were alone, so by staying I had Frank's best interest at heart.

I heard his car door slam, a little louder than normal. I leaned back on the couch with my arm around Gabriella's bare shoulder. I was trying to figure how to bring up my concerns, when her lips began softly kissing my neck and her long fingers stroking my thigh.

I was cooked. She stood up, took me by the hand, and led me to the bedroom.

# Chapter 34

We were lying quietly on top of her sheets when she snuggled next to me. "Anthony, Frank doesn't trust me. Do you? Do you trust me?"

It was the perfect opportunity to ask what else she knew. Clearly, Vitorio was aware of Dino's involvement and had invested knowing they were insuring unhealthy people. But, was Tim Ryan acting on his own or just doing Vitorio's bidding. Was George forced to be involved because of gambling debts or was he a willing participant from the start? Who else would we find in the mix?

What would any good man say with a soft luscious body lying naked in his arms? "Of course I trust you, why wouldn't I?" I said.

She snuggled closer. "I wouldn't blame you if you didn't. I had to hide the truth. I had to protect my uncle."

I really didn't know what I thought about the truth. I waited, hoping she'd volunteer more.

"What do you think we should do, Anthony, now that it seems Frank is safe?"

I tried not to react, but had to wonder why she now felt Frank was safe.

"Do you really think you should get your friend on the police force involved? She has obligations to her job. The more you tell her, the more you create an official structure, which limits the methods of bringing this affair to a conclusion."

I couldn't remember ever mentioning Sonja. Had Gabriella overheard a phone call?

She was rubbing my chest in soft circles as she spoke. "Frank is going to meet with Doctor Bradley, who's an ordinary man with financial problems trying to hang on to his lifestyle. He deleted some notes from the records of a few patients who are friends. They'll collect money from a big bad insurance company. He's devoted his life to helping others. We don't want him to go to jail do we? After Frank talks to him he'll stop, and no one else will get insured. "

The circles were getting larger. Her fingers, reaching lower and lower. I was having difficulty thinking clearly.

Then it struck me. Gabriella wasn't just having a casual conversation. She was like a defense attorney making a carefully rehearsed case to the jury.

I had to agree, for more reasons than one. I replied, my voice now barely a whisper, "No, if I were responsible for him being caught in a scandal, I'd feel terrible."

"Tell Frank," was all I heard, before passion again trumped reason.

This woman, whom I had been obsessing over for five days, was now controlling my thoughts. Frank had said something about a man being no match for an average woman, and that Gabriella was not average. He was right; I was living proof.

# Chapter 35

I woke in darkness, my mind replaying our discussion about Doc Bradley. Gabriella was a lot more involved in this business than she let on and I didn't have the courage to confront her. That ice-cold manipulation she could summon up at any time made me wonder if her passion could be turned on or off, as well. If so, what was her ultimate plan for me?

I decided to not wake her. I slid carefully out of bed, grabbed my clothes and tiptoed downstairs. I called a cab; the dispatcher said ten minutes. There was a note pad on the desk. I printed in large block letters and left it on the table.

Gone to Palm Beach to get the car. Love you very much, Anthony."

Once on the road, I dialed Frank. He answered quickly.

"Have you seen Bradley?"

"No, I'm on my way now."

"What do you plan to say? Are you going to scare him off, or threaten to tell?"

"That will depend on him. I'm going to feed him enough of what I know to get him to open up. If that doesn't work, I'll threaten."

"It would be nice if he'd open up, and we could close this thing down and leave him out of it. He's just a guy in the middle. Doesn't look like they've killed anyone or need to. All the people they insured, and kept, were close to dying anyway."

"Jesus, Tony! Is that what she told you to say? They've got four million on me and I'm not 'close to dying anyway.' She's just trying to protect her uncle. Maybe she's protecting herself. My money says she's in this up to her eyeballs. Possibly Bradley told Maguire's family he had a bad heart to cover up the so-called accident? Who knows what their plan is for people who own coverage and aren't sick. Like me! If it's Bradley or me, he's going down."

Keeping Frank safe and protecting Gabriella was becoming a major conflict. I needed time to think. "Call me when you get out."

I sat for a moment to think it through. It seemed that, when this all began, Ryan was just selling policies to anyone who would buy, some healthy, some unhealthy. The plan was to sell the unhealthy insured to Vitorio's group, and the others through normal channels. If Frank was healthy, maybe his policy got sold to a big reinsurance company and he was safe. Ryan would know but he definitely wasn't telling me. Did Gabriella know? Would she or could she help if needed?

I picked up my car on Clematis and headed for the Marriott to check out. By now Ryan would have talked with Dino and known we were onto their game. They were probably trying to figure how to cover their tails, maybe trying to reach Vitorio.

If they hadn't actually killed anyone, their only problem would be with Gibraltar. They could settle quietly with Gibraltar, who wouldn't want the scandal. A scheme to kill people for their life insurance wasn't exactly great publicity for Gibraltar. Still, someone had already collected on several policies for four or five million apiece. It would be tough to give that back.

I had packed, checked out of the Marriott, and just walked into my room at the Brazilian when the phone rang. I threw my bag on the bed and pulled out the cell. I didn't recognize the number. Maybe Frank was calling from the clinic.

"Hello, Anthony. Tim Ryan. We need to talk."

I waited for him to continue.

"Where can we meet? I'll be in Palm Beach in 30 minutes."

"The bar at Cucina. Nine o'clock."

He hung up. Nine on a Wednesday night, there'd be a big crowd.

I dialed Frank's phone. "Frank, I got a call from Tim Ryan. I'm meeting him at Cucina at nine. Call me."

# Chapter 36

I parked behind Cucina near Publix supermarket and cut through the narrow alley. The back section behind the bar was full. A side door between the buildings leads in past the kitchen and back dining room to the bar up front. It enabled me to see Ryan before he saw me. Sure enough, he was sitting at the semicircular bar between the front and back dining sections. He was facing the front door and hostess station. He turned when he saw me, and then nodded to a table outside.

I sat facing his dark eyes and scowl, the widow's peak and crew cut I'd made fun of.

Without even a hello, he started in, "As you may have discovered from your girlfriend, I have some very convincing people in my camp."

I guessed this meant his threats would be backed up by Vitorio.

Gabriella had claimed her uncle was a gentle and honest man, and Mimi, while not suggesting honest and gentle had said rough stuff wasn't his thing.

I decided to call his bluff. I smiled and nodded.

The scowl now wrinkled his forehead and expanded his cheeks, accentuating the size of his already wide face. "We're prepared to offer you a deal to walk away."

I decided to play along. "What's the deal?"

"I've done some checking on you. You're straight with your friends and clients, but not so straight that you are above breaking into my office; so I'm going to show you how to make some money and protect your pal Frank.

I nodded, but kept silent.

"First, we cancel the policy on Frank and take the hit for the premium loan. Second, we pay you two hundred thousand in cash for the list and your assurance of absolute silence."

He was looking at me for a response. I now knew they owned Frank's policy. Did they know something about his health I didn't? I decided to let him wait. After about a minute, he stood and pointed a finger at my chest. "You know who my partners are. You know they can deliver absolute silence without paying you a penny. I spoke with them this morning. They agree to the terms. I've been told to call at nine tomorrow with your answer. You've got eleven hours to get back to me." He paused, and stared at me, again waiting for a response. When none came he continued. "After that, it's out of my hands."

My new pal, Tim, threw his card on the table, turned, and trotted across the street to the passenger side of that same BMW.

As I walked back inside, Frank was coming though the kitchen area.

"Sorry. I spent more time with Bradley than I intended." He waved me to an empty table, sat down, and leaned his elbows and forearms on the starched table cloth. "I almost felt sorry for the Doc. When I told him we knew about Dino, he was in shock. He didn't seem to know about the list or Vitorio's involvement, so I didn't elaborate.

George, who's been Doc's patient since he was a child, knew about his financial problems and offered him an easy solution. He

guaranteed no one would get hurt, except the insurance company. Said it would only be one or two mutual friends who George
said needed financial help. Doc'd be doing his friends a favor and
solving his own problems as well. When George kept coming with
more files, Bradley got nervous and wanted to stop. George told
him he couldn't or they'd all be caught. He swears Maguire had a
bad heart, and the accident was just that."

Frank flagged down the young blonde waitress. "Honey, I'd like
the veal chop, medium rare, and a Pino Grigio."

He turned back to me. "Bradley was telling the truth. He was
almost relieved to talk to me."

I waved the waitress off. I hadn't eaten, but was far from hungry. "Now what?"

"Doc Bradley will stop changing the medical records and he'll
talk to Dino. He said Dino was getting antsy about the whole
thing anyway, but was afraid of quitting for reasons Doc didn't
understand."

I nodded. "Like threats from Ryan that Vitorio wouldn't be
pleased. Does this mean the operation of insuring the living dead
is shut down?"

The waitress had brought Frank's veal. He was busy eating, I
looked out at the bar. It was filling up, mainly kids. The evening
mating dance between men and women, rich and poor was starting,
and would run till about two. I nodded toward the young couple
that had just sat down at the next table. She had a small nose, rose-
bud lips, short blonde hair and pure alabaster skin. She sat very tall
in her chair and was dressed in Lilly Pulitzer pink. The man was
short; his bare arms were covered with tattoos. His open collared
shirt hinted that his chest and back were covered as well. His shirt,
shorts and sneakers were early Morgan Memorial. Lilly Pulitzer

seemed enchanted. "How much you want to bet her parents told her not to date him, and that's when she got real interested?"

Frank shook his head. "That's not Palm Beach. That's kids."

"Let me tell you about my meeting with Ryan. I was given an ultimatum. He said if I back off, your policy gets cancelled and I get two hundred big ones in cash. If not, it's curtains."

"Do you believe him?"

I picked up the cell and pressed speed dial. "Hello honey, could Ryan have spoken to your uncle this morning?" I held the phone out so Frank could hear.

She hesitated a few seconds, then said, "Not a chance, he's been undergoing tests all morning at a clinic. No cell phones in the hospital."

"Thanks. I'll call you back."

I turned back to Frank. "Ryan's bluffing. He told me he spoke to Vitorio this morning."

"So Tony, let's assume she is telling the truth for once, where does that leave me? Ryan says he'll cancel my policy, but he can't? Gabriella's got to get Uncle Vitorio involved before I'll feel comfortable. So what if there are larger policies out there? Four million is a lot of dough." It was clear from his tone he was annoyed by my using Gabriella as an expert witness.

"Frankie, look, no one's been killed, their group has already collected major money, and they still own policies on a bunch of people with big time health problems. If you insure an average group of seventy-five- to eighty-five-year-olds and wait until they die, you'll make eight to ten percent on your money. If you have an inside track and insure all unhealthy people you make thirty percent or more on your money. That's a pretty good return with no risk. Their best play is to stand pat and wait for the money to come in."

"So, Mr. Know-it-all, what do we do now? Gabriella, who you know wouldn't lie, has assured you that I'm safe and we should forget the whole thing. How involved is George? I think he left Gabriella's with Ryan and Freddie Spring voluntarily. He's in this up to his eyeballs. Now Ryan is beginning to think he's Vitorio. How long before he starts acting like him? You better push her for the truth."

I picked up the cell and dialed her number. "Hi honey, want some company?"

The slight delay in her reply made me a little uncomfortable. Finally, she said, "Of course, how soon will you be here?"

"Soon as I can drive down."

With a self-satisfied smile I said, "The sacrifices I make for our friendship."

"Get some real information, Tony. Push her to talk with the uncle. I know you're in love, or lust, or whatever it is, but there's a lot she's not telling. Tell her Sonja is running her own quiet investigation, which I'm sure is true, and that you can't keep Sonja at bay forever."

I smiled and nodded in agreement, but I had convinced myself that with Vitorio out of commission and Ryan bluffing, Frank and I were safe. Still, to appease Frank I would make an honest effort to get the truth.

# Chapter 37

Driving down A1A, I thought about Frank's knack for reading people, and wondered if he was right. This time I was determined to confront Gabriella, see if she was hiding anything. In the past, every time I tried, she got naked. Not that I was complaining. I've had worse distractions, but she was definitely hiding something.

Now I was worried for Frank. Someone owned a four million dollar policy on his life. That's enough money to create a lot of temptation. I had allowed Gabriella to avoid answering my questions by playing to my male ego, making me feel I was driving her crazy with passion. Time for a new tactic, but what?

I parked in the drive to the left of the house, then thought again. Maybe the boys would return. I drove two blocks toward the center, took a right, parked, locked the car, and walked back to her house.

"Anthony, what did you do with your car?" she asked. Her voice was quiet, she sounded sad. She looked like she might have been crying. I held her chin in my fingers and lifted her head slightly to look more directly into her eyes. "Is everything OK?"

She stared back for a second and then looked down. "I was on the phone about Vitorio. He…" She stopped, then smiled and took my hand. "Come. Let's enjoy each other. No sad talk." She was wearing a light blue silk slip that clung in the heat. I kissed her softly on the lips and felt again that warm firm body against mine, but I forced myself to pull away.

She had opened a bottle of Chianti, from a vineyard I didn't recognize, and poured me a glass. We sat on the couch, our heads back and our feet on the coffee table where she had first shown me the photographs of her family. That night now seemed like ancient history.

I wasn't sure where to start. "Gabriella, I need to understand some things. What was your father's name?"

"Roberto."

"No, his last name."

She hesitated, then answered with a question. "Why? Because my mother was a Giacometti? My mother wanted me to keep the name of her father."

I stood up, walked to the bookshelf where she kept the photo album. I brought it to the couch and placed it on our laps as she had that first night. There was the five-year-old standing between two men. The photo had been enlarged, it covered the full page. The faces were quite clear. I looked again at her, then at her uncle, and then her father.

She reached across her chest, grasped my bicep and squeezed. "I know what you are going to say Anthony, so let me explain. Some of this I was told and some I guessed. That's why I had that photo enlarged several years ago, when my mother was ill with cancer. I brought it to her and she told me this: She was a nineteen-year-old college student on Christmas break, skiing in Davos when she met a very handsome ski instructor."

I thought about Mimi's description of her meeting Vitorio, many years ago in Chicago.

She continued. "They were madly in love, and she became pregnant. My grandfather was furious, and refused to allow her to see Vitorio, let alone marry him. My grandfather was from the old school and had already planned on her marrying the son of his art dealer, which she did. The dealer was visited by Vitorio's family and a deal was struck. They would remain married in name only. Fortunately for me my surrogate father was a very kind and loving man. My childhood was perfect. I never suspected until I was an adult; well, maybe I did, but I loved my father and didn't want to face the truth until long after he died. So, what you suspect is true. Vitorio is my real father. I know this from my mother, but I never told him that I knew."

"Why wouldn't you?"

"You have to understand my uncle. He is very proud, old school, very Italian. He would be embarrassed by this. Plus, our relationship has been established. We love each other as much as is possible. Niece and uncle, daughter and father, what does it matter?"

I shrugged. Growing up with care and guidance of two fathers may have added to her wisdom and strong sense of self-worth. She was right. What did it matter?

Later, would I find it mattered a lot? Once again, had she bought me off with a small piece of the truth?

Her grip on my arm had loosened, so I put my arm around her and pulled her close. "Gabriella, Frank spoke to Doc Bradley. He was terrified when he realized Frank knew what they were up to. Doc told Frank how George had set it up, convinced him he was helping friends, and said no one would get hurt. Doc promised he would stop falsifying records, and begged Frank to keep his secret. Frank inferred he would, but didn't promise anything."

She was listening intently. "Did Bradley know who else was involved?"

"You mean like, Vitorio?" I had hesitated, not sure whether to say uncle or father. "I think Bradley's only dealt with George and Dino. He doesn't seem to know Ryan personally at all."

She looked at me as though expecting more. Her eyes had lost their redness. Had she had bad news about Vitorio's health?

When I was silent, she asked, "Are you comfortable now that Frank is safe? He's why you got involved in the first place."

"I guess you're in a better position to find out if he's safe than I. I believe the unhealthy insureds are steered by Ryan to Vitorio's group, the others are sold elsewhere. We assume Frank is in the healthy group. Am I right? Is Frank safe?"

"What do you mean? No one has been killed. Everyone died a natural death. If both groups are holding the policies and waiting for time and aging to do its natural work, why does it matter to Frank who owns the policy?"

I had debated with myself whether to tell her about Ryan's threat to me. I decided to wait. Instead, I countered with, "Just because Vitorio is playing it straight doesn't mean Ryan is."

She tried to act surprised, but I sensed she wasn't when she said a little too innocently, "You think that Ryan would kill for the insurance money?"

I hesitated, then said, "There's a lot of money involved, and people like my friend Sonja will eventually figure out what's going on. Ryan and others involved may not have time to wait for natural deaths."

Gabriella sat up abruptly, "And Vitorio might be implicated."

I thought about Frank's comment that Vitorio hadn't been seen for some time and asked, "Exactly how is Vitorio's health?"

She stared at me for a long minute, as though considering telling me some secret, and then said, "He's had surgery."

She took my two hands in hers. "Anthony, I know you are too much of a gentleman to ask, so I will tell you. George and I were friends, never lovers."

I wasn't sure if that was to distract me or not, but it felt good.

I waited for more on Vitorio, and when it didn't come, I looked at my watch. It was after eleven. I put my arms around her and said, "You look tired. Ready for bed?"

She stood and stretched like a cat before a nap. "Come, let's see if you can let me sleep."

I followed her upstairs. We slept, eventually.

# Chapter 38

I woke early as usual, first thinking about Ryan's threat to get back to him by nine, then sat watching Gabriella as she slept. She was on her side facing me, her toned arms, slim waist and gorgeous breasts only half covered by the sheet. Her tanned skin had the essence of a woman half her age. She was breathing easily; I decided to let her sleep.

Hoping she'd still be in bed upon my return, I tiptoed down the stairs, dressed, and walked the few blocks to the center of town. The local coffee shop was already busy. I grabbed a half-cafe with milk, picked up the Palm Beach Post and settled at the end of the long counter. As I was finishing the sports section, I tuned in to the conversation of two men next to me. One was discussing the traumas of divorce. I assumed from the way he went into details the two were close friends. Sensing I had overheard at least the drift of the conversation, the listener put his arm around the victim's shoulder, winked at me and said loud enough for all to hear, "It just proves my theory about women. Sometimes, the f---in you get ain't worth the f---in you get." I nodded. I understood, but not from personal experience.

I glanced at my watch, 8:15. Between reading the paper and hearing the divorce details, I'd been gone almost two hours. On the walk back to Gabriella's I thought about the conversation I'd overheard, and felt a little defensive about my own marriage and relationships. I'd concluded some time ago that any problems I'd had with women or life in general were self induced. The extension of that has to be that I had caused grief for others. That bothered me.

Still deep in thought, I had stepped into the kitchen when it dawned on me, I'd walked up the driveway beside the house and hadn't seen Gabriella's car. I opened the front door and looked out at the driveway. Sure enough, it was gone.

My first reaction was panic. I wasn't sure if my panic was from fear she'd been abducted by Ryan and company, or that she'd left me. Then I saw a note on the counter, in her perfect handwriting:

Dear Anthony,

It's Vitorio. I have to go to him. I will call you soon. I promise.

Love, Gabriella

The "Love, Gabriella" was somewhat comforting, but why hadn't she waited, or at least been more specific about why she had to leave immediately? I ran upstairs; the bed was made, everything was picked up. The closet, normally full, was half-empty and the top two drawers in her bureau, where women keep underwear, socks and jerseys, was cleaned out. This was planned the day before, maybe earlier. Her hesitation when I called her from Cucina? She knew then. I ran back down, two steps at a time. Maybe she had called from the car and left a message on my cell. It was on the table where we'd been sitting the night before. I switched it on. No calls.

I was getting annoyed.

I called Frank. No answer, not unusual. "I'm at Gabriella's, she left unexpectedly, her uncle's ill. Call me."

I ran the two blocks to my car and headed back to Palm Beach. On the way I called Palm Beach International, and asked about flights to Chicago. There was one flight on United at 8:50. To clear security she'd have had to get there at 8:00 and have left the house by 7:15. I left at 6:30. In order to pack, dress and drive to the airport she'd have to have gotten up right after I left. She had to have known last night she was leaving. Something was very wrong.

As I approached Palm Beach my phone rang. It was Frank. "Tony, I told you not to trust that broad. Where are you?"

"A1A, just south of Mar-a-Lago."

"Meet me at Hamburger Heaven."

I hung up. I was not emotionally ready to give up on her. I knew she put Vitorio first, but I couldn't come to grips with the idea that the passion we'd shared was just that, passion, with no feelings of love attached. She'd shown interest from that first night we flirted, long before she knew who I was. She'd asked Mrs. Fisher and others about me. She'd shared the secret with me about her father that even he didn't know.

It didn't seem possible that she'd double cross me. Nothing made sense.

I entered through the glass door, and scanned the oval bar. No Frank. I headed down to the last booth before the kitchen and sat facing the door.

Frank waved at the door, lumbered over, then plopped down in the booth opposite me. I was expecting a lecture or general dissertation on women. Instead, it was, "Well Tony, what do you think is going on?"

I shrugged, half feeling guilty that I'd let her manipulate me, and half not knowing if she had. "I assume she's gone to Chicago."

"That's pretty quick planning, don't you think? She must have known she was leaving last night, or earlier. What did she take for clothes? Did you check?"

"Yes. She took more than a quick trip's worth."

Frank was waving the waitress over. It was Sarah, my friend who used to tend bar at Cucina's. He gave her a big smile. "Too early for one of those great hamburgers, medium rare, with lettuce and tomato?"

I wondered why Frank never put on weight. He ate like a longshoreman.

Sarah nodded, made a note on her pad, and looked at me.

"Just coffee is fine, Sarah. Thanks."

Frank was quiet for a minute then said, "Call Sonja. See if she can get the passenger list for the Chicago flight."

I called, hoping his suspicions were wrong, but not to call Sonja would seem like I was covering for Gabriella. Plus, I was starting to have some doubts of my own.

"Hi baby, where you been? You deserted me for that savvy little Milano chick."

"Sorry, things have been a bit crazy. Can you check a plane passenger list for me?"

"What's the deal?"

"That savvy little number left this morning, apparently to see her uncle in Chicago. He's sick, or having tests, or something."

"You're not sure she's on that flight?" She hesitated, "Why? No, tell me later. I have a friend at the airport who has access to the manifests. I'll call you right back."

Frank, who was listening while making short work of his all-beef breakfast, managed to stop eating long enough to hold up his wallet. "I'll bet you ten bucks she's not on that flight."

I was afraid he was right, but in defense of the woman I loved, I nodded.

Feeling a little hollow, I tried to smile. "Should we tell Sonja about Ryan's threat, and your conversation with Doc Bradley?"

"I'd leave Doc Bradley out of it for now. Tell her about Ryan. He's a loose cannon. Don't discount his doing something crazy on his own."

Sonja called back, "Gabriella's not on that flight. So I had my friend trace her by name. She's booked on a Delta 10:20 a.m. flight to Atlanta, then a 3:45 flight to Rome by way of Paris, all first class." She paused, like she knew the answer, "Are there some things you're not telling me?"

She must have known by my silence that I was as surprised as she. "She said her uncle was sick, but we assumed he's in Chicago." I looked over at Frank, who was holding out his big paw for the ten bucks.

"Where are George and Ryan?" Sonja said. "Yesterday morning you were heading down to see her, thinking she may have been in trouble."

She was too good a friend to play games. I looked over at Frank and mouthed Tim Ryan. He nodded. I told her about meeting with Tim Ryan last night at Cucina.

Sonja was laughing.

"I'm getting death threats and you're laughing?"

"Sorry, it just strikes me as funny. Frank is getting killed for his insurance; you're getting a couple hundred grand for going back to Boston. Your girlfriend says her favorite uncle is dying in Chicago, but she's really on a Roman holiday. What next?"

I decided to give her a real "what's next."

"One more thing. I asked Gabriella why her last name was Giacometti which is her mother's last name. It turns out Vitorio is her real father."

I could hear Sonja gasp on the other end of the line. Her reply, not what I expected, was, "This is really weird. I was just reading a police report about the Italian Mafia and the emergence of women in their ranks. Some families have been feuding for decades. So many husbands, fathers and sons have been killed the surviving wives, mothers, and daughters have had to take over to seek revenge. They're often more vicious than the men. Do you suppose your friend is in Rome on a hit?"

I hoped she was just kidding. I couldn't picture that sweet soft body doing anything but making love.

"Possibly." Was all I could muster. "She said Vitorio's in Chicago. Is there any way you can check on that?"

"Maybe. There's a guy with the FBI in Lauderdale who has always liked me. They keep an eye on Mafia figures; maybe he can find out where the uncle or daddy, or whatever he is, is. I'll call you back."

Suddenly I was hungry. I waved to Sarah.

"Hi sweetie, you want a burger like your pal?"

I nodded. Somehow I didn't feel like talking. Frank must have sensed how down I was over the possibility I had been played by Gabriella. He got up, walked to the front of the restaurant and picked up a newspaper. He sat back down, raised the paper, and left me alone with my thoughts.

I thought again about Gabriella's hesitation when I had called from Cucina. At the time I'd felt like she didn't want me to come over, and now I knew why. She knew she was leaving in the morning. She let me come anyway. Did she mean to tell me more and decided not to?

"Here's your hamburger, sweetie, medium rare. I remembered."

Sarah had a half smile. I had to admit she had beautiful eyes, very cute girl, with that kind Midwestern disposition and a great body. I mean, if you like that sort of thing.

"You in town for long? I'm still at the Palm Beach Hotel."

"I'm working on a fairly involved case. If I get some free time, we'll have lunch." I figure the suggestion for lunch rather than dinner would send a message. She smiled as though it didn't. Go figure. I guess we all filter things out and hear what we want. I wondered if I was doing that with Gabriella.

Frank had dropped his paper and was watching me. He knew I was struggling with Gabriella thoughts, and was trying to read whether he should kid, lecture, give fatherly advice, or stay out of it.

He chose the latter. "Very nice girl," he said, nodding to Sarah. "You been out with her?"

"Not really, just a little flirting."

The phone interrupted our conversation. It was Sonja.

Her voice was a little higher pitched than normal. "It's not my friend's case so his information is old, but as far as he knows, Vitorio dropped out of sight over a month ago. They think he could have left the country, but he hasn't been seen in Italy or Switzerland where he has homes."

Frank had noticed my expression and was motioning me to tell him what was going on. "Hold on, Sonja," I relayed the message to Frank, then spoke again to Sonja. "Why would Gabriella make up a story about him being sick in Chicago?" I was feeling duped. "Why would he leave town? Was he being charged with something?"

"No," she continued, "that's the crazy part. He's been laying low for years now. He's donated money to local causes in Chicago, owns several legitimate businesses, and is respected and even admired in the community. Course there's always a fascination with these Mafia types. They want people to believe they are legitimate, but he's pulled it off. In some ways he's no different from a lot of America's richest families who made their money by questionable means and now are known by the family foundation. Every time there's a problem with a school or elderly housing, he's been like Robin Hood to the rescue. I doubt you could find enough people in the whole city to make up a jury that would convict him of anything. Where he's gone is a mystery."

I was pleased to hear the positive stuff. It legitimized my feeling about Gabriella and her concern for his reputation, but why had she lied? To protect him when he is ill and vulnerable?

"Sounds probable," I said. "Maybe that's why she's going to Rome."

"I know you have a thing for this woman, Tony, but something doesn't smell right." She was silent for a moment. "One more thing, my friend in Lauderdale told me on the QT. Those body parts on the beach. Italian Mafia, like from Italy. Please be careful. Got to go, staff meeting. Keep me posted," she said and hung up.

I looked at Frank.

He smiled. "Anthony, I haven't seen you this smitten, ever. You got two choices. Go after her. Or forget her. You'll drive yourself crazy sitting around picking petals off daisies with this she-loves-me she-loves-me-not bit. Go to Rome; find out."

Frank had a knack for getting to the heart of things. No pun intended. He knew me better than I knew myself. He was right. I loved her. I needed to find out the truth. I had to know if what we had was real.

I picked up the phone. Could I get to Atlanta in time for that Paris-Rome flight?

# Chapter 39

I got lucky. The woman booking my flight was in Tampa, not Bombay. If I caught the 12:55 from West Palm, I'd arrive in Atlanta at 2:45 and have about an hour to find my connecting flight at 3:45 to Paris. For anyone not familiar with the Atlanta airport, an hour may seem like plenty of time, but this place covers the equivalent of forty-five football fields. With north and south terminals and five concourses, it can be confusing. Fortunately it has a very efficient underground train system called a People Mover. I had instructions as to exactly where to go and what car to take for the flight transfer.

I was sprinting down Concourse E with about ten minutes to spare when it dawned on me, I still didn't know what I would say to Gabriella when caught up with her. "Oh, hi honey, funny running into you on a flight to Paris, five hundred miles from the bed where we made love last night." I slowed to a walk. Most passengers had boarded. I was economy; she'd be in first class. Fortunately we were entering through the center door. I didn't have to walk through first class. Time to think.

The flight attendant at the door must have thought I was crazy. I peeked around the side of the bulkhead to see where Gabriella was seated. I didn't want to be seen until I half knew what was going on. She was standing in the aisle close to the front of the plane talking to a man placing a pink carry-on bag in the overhead rack, clearly not his. Gabriella slid in first and sat by the window. I could see from the size of her escort's shoulders he was rather large. I wished I could call Sonja and see if those two had booked together, but I was embarrassed enough to be doing what I was doing. I was getting feelings of being in high school, spying on a girlfriend who had just dumped me, and wondering if I should have come at all. I smiled at the attendant, whose badge said "Sherry." She'd been watching me closely, probably thought I was either a pervert or a terrorist.

"I thought I recognized an old girlfriend."

She smiled. "If she's the lady in 2A, too bad she's an 'ex.' That is a very classy lady."

I decided not to say more and headed back to my seat, which was halfway back on the left.

Needing time to think, I tried not to make eye contact with the unattractive couple next to me. It didn't work. They gleefully began explaining, in alternate sentences, that they would be married five years that coming weekend. They planned to spend their anniversary in a hotel on the Rue de Rivoli, hopefully in the same bed where they had honeymooned.

I've stayed near the Louvre and Tuileries Gardens. It is a beautiful spot. I wasn't sure if I was better off saying I had been there and risk their wanting to discuss it, or say I hadn't and have them need to describe it. I decided to change the subject.

"Do you have children?"

The gentleman quickly opened his wallet and pushed a photo of a miniature poodle in my face. I held the photo and examined it closely.

Now, I've got no problem with dogs, but they are not children. I couldn't help myself. "Wow," I said, "if that's your child, you must have really interesting sex."

It worked. He snatched back the photo and decided to leave me alone.

I was getting nervous; instead of intercepting Gabriella and convincing her to include me in whatever her adventure might be, I was now sneaking along, following her. The longer I trailed Gabriella without making contact, the more difficult explaining my being here would become. I concocted a plan and hoped that the nice flight attendant would help.

I waited until the curtain between coach and first class was closed and Sherry was alone, then walked up and pretended to be going to the lavatory. When Sherry was clearly watching me I pulled aside the curtain and gazed longingly at my "ex." Then I closed the curtain and looked down.

"Still carrying a torch?" She asked softly. "That's tough. My husband left me after seven years. I thought everything was fine be-tween us and, bang, I came home from a trip and he was gone. Ran off with an old girlfriend whom he'd done nothing but complain about. Go figure."

"Oh, I'm sorry. Was this recent?"

"About a year now. I guess that's what that seven year-itch thing is about. I'm pretty much over it, but it was hard. I know what you're going through." She had placed her hand on my arm, trying to comfort me. I decided to enlist her help.

"To tell you the truth," I began, "we had a big fight just before she left. I decided to surprise her by coming on the trip. You can imagine my shock when I got to the airport and saw her with this other guy." She had her hand on my shoulder now. My sad tale seemed to be working.

Sherry patted my back. "Let me see what I can find out for you," she said. Pushing the curtain aside, she walked toward the front, where the other flight attendants were mixing drinks. The restroom was vacant; I decided to wait in there.

Sure enough, in no time flat there was a knock on the door. "Mr. Tauck?" I opened the door and stepped out.

She pulled the curtain tight, as though she were now a part of my conspiracy, and bent toward me to whisper, "Good news. The girls don't think they're a couple; just traveling together. He's very attentive, maybe he'd like it to be more, but that's not what is going on." She patted my arm again.

I made a mental note to always fly Delta. "Is there any way I could get a message to her, without her knowing I'm on the plane?"

"That's kind of tough, but we could have a message waiting when she gets off in Paris. The pilot's a great guy, I'm sure we could get him to call ahead."

"Boy, you sure do have a lot of power." I said, wanting to show I was impressed.

She smiled and blushed, "He's my new boyfriend."

I gave her a hug. "And here I was feeling sorry for you. I should have known you're too nice to be free for very long. I'll write up a message. We've got another four hours."

I headed back and sat down with the honeymooners.

I wondered, is the big guy working for Vitorio, and bringing her to see him? He's a bodyguard; Vitorio's in hiding?

My thoughts were being interrupted by a sick feeling in my gut. Was our romance just part of a game she was playing?

I had begun to think of the future as our future. I'd had this feeling for a woman only once before and that woman I married. I'd been in love or thought I'd been in love several times since, but it was just my old habit of confusing love and lust. This time, even though our sex was as natural as breathing, there was a lot more to my relationship with Gabriella.

I began to write:

Dearest Gabriella,

I was worried about you, and called the airport. A friendly agent told me you were flying to Paris, not Chicago. Are you alright? Please call me on my cell.

With love and concern,
Anthony

Feeling pleased with myself, I sat looking at my note when Sherry showed up.

She squatted next to me, "I think she knows you're here."

"How?" I stammered. "How could she know? She never saw me get on the plane."

"I asked the girls in front to keep an eye on her. They said she made several long calls on the plane's pay phone. I was there when she got off the last call. She opened the curtain between first and coach and stared down the aisle in your direction. Someone she spoke to by phone must have told her something. I watched her when she sat back down. She seemed concerned, almost sad."

Oh my God, I thought, maybe she's sad that she has to have me killed. Talk about the good news and the bad news.

I turned to my friend and, I hoped, my protector, "What do you think I should do? Did it seem as though she had discussed it with her escort?"

"I don't think so. She got off the phone and walked straight back to look. There wasn't any conversation when she sat back down."

I had to take a chance. I had to see her, tell her how I felt, talk about our future. Find out if we had one.

I scribbled a quick note. "Meet me in the lavatory between first and coach, on your side, in three minutes. Love you, Anthony." I folded it once, and handed it to my new friend and accomplice. "Could you give her this note?"

She gave me a big smile. I was turning a routine flight into a soap opera. It would keep the girls talking for weeks. She stood up and hurried down the aisle. I knew as soon as Sherry hit the first class cabin she'd open and read it. That was fine. Maybe having them watching me was my "just in case" protection.

I got up, trying to look casual. I was far from it. I stepped into the bathroom, closed the door, and slid the bolt to lock the door and turn on the "occupied" sign.

Like a nervous kid in the principal's office, wanting to kill time, I felt compelled to wipe the sink and shelf, to tidy up for my visitor. Cleaning up is completely out of character for me.

As I was trying to gather my thoughts, find the words to describe my feelings, my hopes, there was a knock on the door. It was loud. Had she sent the bodyguard?

I slowly slid back the lock and pushed the door aside. Like a thief entering a strange home, her head was slightly bowed, her eyes looking at the floor. I ushered Gabriella in with a gentle tug on her forearm. The confined space brought us close. I had to lean against her, and reach over her shoulder, to slide the door bolt. I smelled just the slightest hint of lavender before she suddenly threw her arms around me and began peppering my neck, cheeks, and lips with tiny kisses. My plan to describe my feelings as mainly of the heart, with lust as a distant second, was soon forgotten. The sudden reversal, from fearing I had lost her, to this concentration of urgent passion brought excruciating pleasure. Abandoning my rehearsed speech, I lifted her to the countertop. Then, still clinging to me, she hiked her skirt and kicked free of her panties. Slowly she slid off the counter and wrapped herself around me, abandoning her body to the moment, our tongues first softly touching then dancing with passion. Finally, exhausted but fulfilled, all movement stopped. I could feel the warmth of her breath on my cheek. We continued to hold each other, our two hearts pounding, in a vise grip of passion and breathlessness, I gently rested her bare bottom back on my newly cleaned counter top. Slowly our faces separated while our bodies remained close. There was a rap on the door. "Are you all right in there?" It sounded like my flight attendant friend.

I released my grip and leaned toward the door. "Be right out."

I turned back to Gabriella who was still sitting on the counter, skirt above her waist, lipstick smeared onto her cheeks, her hair in disarray. She began to laugh like a kid in school who doesn't want to get caught laughing. The more she tried to control it, the more it came. Finally she stopped, hopped down, and adjusted her skirt.

Clearly embarrassed by her involuntary display of passion, she turned toward the wash basin to avoid looking me in the eye. She was first to speak. "I'd better clean up or they'll know what we were doing."

I had a feeling Sherry already knew what we "were doing," but, not wanting to add to Gabriella's embarrassment, I didn't reply. She was cleaning up in the sink with her back to me.

"Did you follow me because you love me, Anthony? You couldn't stand to be without me for even a day?"

I smiled at her reflection in the mirror and patted her now-covered fanny. "I hope you know how I feel," I said tenderly.

Gabriella turned and faced me, then put her arms around my neck and gave me the softest kiss. A kiss of love, not passion. I wondered.

Gabriella pulled open the latch and stepped into the doorway still facing me and said, "You remember our first night together? What I told you?"

She stood for a moment waiting for my reply, when none came, she turned and walked back to her seat. Watching her leave was as though I were looking at her through the wrong end of a telescope. Was this it for us?

Sherry gave me a wink and thumbs up and whispered, "Welcome to the mile-high club."

I was glad Gabriella couldn't hear.

I walked back and joined the newlyweds, who, fortunately, were still not speaking to me. I had planned to tell Gabriella I loved her, wanted to spend my life with her, instead I had succumbed again to her passion, again never explained how I felt.

Physically exhausted, and mentally confused, I tipped back my seat.

Surrendering to drowsiness, I tried to remember what it was that she told me that first night.

# Chapter 40

I slept. How long or how well, I didn't know until I heard the pilot making an announcement in French, which my half-awake mind caught the second time around. We were descending into de Gaulle International.

I stayed seated until I saw Gabriella and her protector heading off the plane. When I stood, a slip of paper fell from my lap. In an exact and block style handwriting it read: "Meet-entrance baggage claim Paris-have plan."

As I left the plane, six female eyes were looking me over closely and three mouths trying to hold polite grins. Sherry had wasted no time in telling her pals about my private get-together with Gabriella. Their smiles turned to giggles when I replied to their "Thank you for flying Delta," with "Thank you! I don't think I've ever enjoyed a flight more."

Once in the airport I saw that everyone was dressed in jackets or sweaters for a typical late March day. My cotton golf shirt wasn't going to hack it. I'd need to pick up some warmer clothes. Even Rome would be cooler than Palm Beach.

I followed the signs for baggage claim as instructed, but something didn't make sense. It was 6:45, the Rome flight was at 7:15. We deplaned in terminal 2B. The Rome flight departed from 2C.

Even with the terminals side by side, that wasn't much time to meet between planes. I picked up the pace.

Concerned she'd be with her bodyguard, I stopped short of my destination and searched the crowd. No sign of her or him. I was feeling both braver and more anxious about the time, so I circled in closer to the waiting crowd. Then a voice behind me called my name, "Anthony, back here." The voice, with an Italian accent was coming from beside the steel lockers outside the rest room. I hesitated, and then walked back. A short, balding man with a large nose and a gold front tooth waved and patted the seat next to him. He held out his large hand to greet me. Up close his nose looked like it had been broken more than once, and above his eyebrow was the scar tissue of a boxer who lost a few.

"Anthony, I am Pasquale Toncarina, a friend of Gabriella's family. She has asked me to look out for you."

I glanced at my watch, 7:02. He placed his hand on my arm and shook his head. "We'll take a later flight."

I started to get up. "No, I should be on this flight with Gabriella."

His grip was firm. "I don't think you understand Anthony. You don't have a choice."

In spite of his calm friendly tone, the idea of missing my flight and losing track of Gabriella made me more than a little uncomfortable. Then I realized it might already be too late. Plus, no one but Gabriella knew I'd be at baggage claim. I had to trust him. I relaxed back into the plastic chair.

He released his grip, and patted my knee. "Trust me. You will see her soon, but not today. There are flights to Rome every two hours. We'll have some breakfast and catch a noon flight."

He stood and waved for me to follow. "Come."

# Chapter 41

The restaurant was elaborately decorated like a French bistro with red velvet booths. Large chandeliers hung from the high ceiling. The hostess walked us through the main dining area to a booth in the back. Red cloth walls and Impressionist paintings added to its upscale atmosphere. Above our booth hung a Degas painting of ballerinas in a heavy gold frame.

With my stomach gently reminding me that I hadn't eaten since Hamburger Heaven, I skimmed the menu. In French, it listed what appeared to be about a dozen omelet and quiche dishes. I was trying to find something I'd recognize and was about to close my eyes and pick a number, when I realized the woman in the next booth, a tall slim woman with short red hair, was trying to get my attention. She smiled and pointed to her plate and asked, "You are American? Try the croque monsieur." Her sharp features and smooth gestures reminded me of the Degas ballerina I had just admired.

I nodded. The waitress, who was watching, smiled and took my menu. Pasquale ordered something I didn't understand, which turned out to be a blend of coffees.

Pasquale smiled his approval, apparently appreciating French women as much as I. "You are a man women feel comfortable with." He pointed a long finger at me and said, "A curse and a blessing." He was about to continue when he suddenly looked over my shoulder and stood up quickly. "Excuse me, there is someone I know." He waved at a tall young man in a belted cashmere top coat, carrying an umbrella. They hugged, kissed on both cheeks and sat at a table near the door. From their animated conversation it appeared they were friends who hadn't seen each other in a while and were catching up. When the second man glanced my way and nodded, I wondered if their meeting had to do with me.

The waitress placed my croque monsieur on the table and left. As she did, the attractive red-head stood up, walked toward me, and whispered in a now distinctly American accent, "You are in dangerous hands, follow me. There is a door in the rear where you can slip out unnoticed."

Was it the American accent, or was it her looks that made me immediately trust her? Whatever it was, I followed without thinking. As she led me though the non-public section of the airport, she introduced herself by pulling out a badge, "Emily Jones, FBI."

Seeing my puzzled look, she said, "I'll explain in a moment. We must hurry."

She led me down a long dark corridor to a steel door, which she unlocked, and we stepped into a large room filled with policemen wearing the tri-color flag of France on their shoulders. Most were seated at a counter against two of the three empty walls, wearing headphones and looking at monitor displays of people in the airport. Emily motioned me to one of the screens, and said something in French to the policeman at the desk. He hit a key and the screen showed Pasquale and his friend in their booth. She pointed to the tall younger man, "This man is the head of a crime family in Sardinia. The other man, Pasquale, works for him. They were going to fly with you to Rome and then, after you cleared customs, instead of taking you to Gabriella, they planned to kidnap you. Their plan was to force Gabriella to make some concessions at the meeting she flew here to attend. You were to be their bargaining chip."

I was trying to get my sleep-deprived brain to compute. "What are you saying? What does Gabriella have to do with those men?"

"She has everything to do with them, Mr. Tauck. Her uncle has been ill for some time. Unexpectedly, he took a turn for the worse and died yesterday. His death has been kept secret from all but a few."

"So what does that have to do with Gabriella?"

"She inherited his position. There has always been speculation that he was her father; this seems to confirm it. She is on her way to a suburb of Rome for her swearing-in ceremony at a meeting of the families in Tuscolano."

"But she's a woman!" I proclaimed more loudly than I intended. I knew that sounded stupid and chauvinistic.

Seeing my discomfort, Emily Jones smiled. "Women are often quite active in Mafia families. Their husbands are killed, and they take over. We believe she has been involved in the Chicago operation for some time. Her father and his lieutenants have been grooming her for the position since she was a teen."

"It can't be; she's so feminine."

Emily smiled, "And dangerous, Mr. Tauck, like a black widow spider. Like the praying mantis that bites off the head of the male after they mate. She was once involved with the younger man in the booth. She tried to kill him, and would have succeeded if not for... Not important now, though this is another reason he wishes to get even."

I shook my head. "Now what?"

"We believe that her father was trying to modernize, basically go legit, and we assume she will continue that trend. It is in our best interest to keep her in power, at least for now. Those who would replace her are old school."

"So, is she going to bite off my head?"

I was kidding; Emily's look said she wasn't. "We don't know. Maybe she likes you. There doesn't seem to be anything she can gain from the relationship, but it does put you at risk."

My thoughts, racing round and round, kept coming up with a contradiction. "You seemed to be able to spirit me away pretty easily. Why didn't Pasquale watch me more closely?"

Emily her raised hands, palms up, as if to say who knows, but followed with, "It didn't matter. I had six plainclothes Paris police close by. We'd have gotten you out either way."

I was wondering if I should continue on to Rome or wait? Emily seemed to know what I was thinking. She was shaking her head. "Going to Rome would be extremely dangerous. We are less able to protect you there. We're sending you back to the States with an escort. You have a flight in the morning."

She turned to an officer at the next counter. "Pierre, would you take Mr. Tauck to the Intercontinental Hotel and stay with him until his morning flight?"

She turned back to me. "Please join me this evening at La Brasserie Lipp."

I scowled at the suggestion that I'd be under Pierre's watchful eye, but smiled and nodded when she mentioned dinner. She was indeed a very intriguing woman. I vaguely hoped she might have more than spying on her mind.

# Chapter 42

After my nap at the Intercontinental, Pierre and I left the hotel and crossed the Rue de Rivoli, where my honeymooning friends with the dog/child were perhaps trying to produce another one. We passed through the Tuileries Gardens, crossed the Seine, and continued on to the Boulevard Saint Germain and La Brasserie Lipp.

Crossing the boulevards in Paris is not the same as in Palm Beach. Cars in Palm Beach often resemble the gondolas of Venice, drifting calmly, the passengers enjoying the sights. In Paris crossing a boulevard is more like crossing the Indi-500 race track.

Pierre, now out of uniform, left me at the door of the restaurant and joined a conversation at the bar. It appeared he knew the bartender and several of the patrons. I guessed he was a regular.

Emily stood when I came in and patted the seat next to her for me to join her French style, where all patrons face the center of the restaurant to see and be seen. She was dressed in a stylish, closely cut dress.

As soon as we ordered drinks, I said, "I assume you are an American, but your looks and mannerisms are so French."

She laughed, "Yes. My father was a graduate student in France where he met my mother. He married her and brought her to the

States. I am American, but speak French and look like my mother. That is why I am posted here."

As soon as the drinks came she was all business. "Mr. Tauck, we need your help."

I turned to face her. "Look Emily, I care very much for Gabriella, and in spite of your praying mantis depiction, I believe she feels the same. I won't do anything against her. If you want help in protecting her, I'm more than happy to comply. Though from what you've told me, she seems quite capable of taking care of herself."

The wine steward opened the bottle of Chateau de Rothschild and poured a small amount in my glass. It was very smooth burgundy. I nodded my approval; he poured our glasses half full and left.

She held her glass to mine. "Sante'. I hope you are right. We are only asking you to keep us in the loop with an occasional call. Remember, we would like her to remain in power and legit."

I took another sip of wine. "No problem, as long as it doesn't compromise my relationship."

Several glasses of wine and an excellent pan-fried Dover sole later, she escorted me back to Pierre. We said goodnight.

Back at the hotel, with Pierre sleeping in the outer room, I tried Gabriella's cell. One ring, then came that clear voice, with its hint of an accent, telling me to leave a message. Hearing her voice brought back visions of our meeting on the plane. I had so much I wanted to say, but not knowing her status, or who might listen in, I said only, "Delayed by your rivals. I'm OK, heading to Palm Beach in the a.m. Call me."

As I nodded off, I wondered if she had a second cell phone with her message in Italian.

# Chapter 43

I didn't think it was possible to get through de Gaulle in less than two hours, but in thirty minutes tops Pierre had us at the gate where he proceeded to escort me to the plane. I wondered if word of my lavatory exploits had prompted all this fuss. Despite my many attempts, Pierre was tight lipped. I may never know how long and how closely the FBI had been watching me.

We arrived in Atlanta a little late and had a couple of hours wait for the flight to West Palm. At ten of seven I was in my car. I checked my phone for messages. There were seven.

A call from Sonja. "Tony, call me immediately." She sounded distressed.

A second call from Sonja. "Tony, it's Frank. He's been in an accident, or at least we are considering it was an accident until we have further proof. He's in JFK Hospital, call me."

Both messages were left this morning; it must have taken a while for them to catch up with my message service. I hit the speed dial for Sonja. No answer. I called JFK. "I'd like information on a patient, Frank Forbes."

The receptionist quickly replied. "Mr. Forbes is in intensive care. Are you immediate family?"

I lied, "Yes, I'm his stepson, Anthony Tauck. I'll be there in thirty minutes."

I pulled over and took a deep breath. I pictured Frank smiling and giving me his patented bear hug at our meeting only a week ago in the Palm Beach Grill. I was again trying to cope with the possibility of his death. He was too full of fun and energy, too important to me to die. I realized that once Gabriella had assured me he wasn't in danger, I'd relaxed my efforts to protect him.

I pulled back into the traffic and headed south on 95. I'm not religious. I had enough Catholicism stuffed down my throat as a kid to last a lifetime, but as I drove, I asked God for help. I thought about Ryan. It had to be him. It couldn't have been done by Vitorio's people. I stopped myself. Here I was still thinking "Vitorio," not "Gabriella."

Definitely not Gabriella. She knew he was my best friend. Besides, Emily said she was following a more modern approach, no more killings. Ryan had to have done it himself, or with that punk Freddie Spring. George also had a lot to gain from Frank's death. No, I thought, he wouldn't have the stomach for it.

I took the Sixth Avenue turnoff, and pulled into the parking lot for JFK. I sat, then after a deep breath, I walked to the front desk. I was directed to the sixth floor, Intensive Care. Visions of Frank flowed through my head: Frank at his wedding, so happy; I could picture him across from me in Green's, laughing as I teased Barbara's daughter Daisy.

"Are you Mr. Tauck?" It was an older nurse with a generous smile. I nodded. She took my hand and spoke as though she were my grandmother. "I must warn you, Mr. Forbes is in a coma. He won't recognize you."

I can't know how long I stood by the bed looking at his pale face, the IV dripping, and thinking how impossible it was that this man who had been such an important part of my life was now so silent. My phone vibrated in my back pocket.

"Are you there at the hospital?" It was Sonya.

"I'm with him now," I whispered stepping out into the hall. "What happened?"

"We're checking his car. Looks like his brake lines were cut, maybe something with the steering. About dusk he was driving down the shore road in South Palm Beach, speeding. He hit a tree. No skid marks. We can't figure where he was going. We suspect he got a phone call and was responding to it. His last call, ten minutes before he crashed, was from guess who?"

I knew. "Tim Ryan."

"Yup. We're looking for him now. The call was from his cell. He could be anywhere." Then she asked, "What happened to Rome?"

"Long story, I'll tell you when I see you. When are you off duty?"

"I'm off. How about a drink? My honey is at a bachelor party."

I looked at my watch. 10:15. "How about that Greek place, Leila's, off Clematis by Ultima Fitness? It stays open late. I'll head there now."

# Chapter 44

The six-person bar was empty except for Sonja.

I said, "It's great to see you," and meant it. The trip to Paris and back in two days, plus seeing Frank, had taken its toll. Sonja's hug felt good, like a mother consoling a tired, cranky eight-year-old.

"Any change in Frank's condition?"

"Still no movement."

She turned in her swivel chair and put her hands on my knees. "What happened with Gabriella? You OK?"

I told her everything, including my apparent rescue by Emily. She was fascinated by that meeting and asked more questions than I had answers for. I omitted the mile-high club, describing it as, "She was clearly happy to see me." By the end of my tale, I was on my third Mykos and getting sleepy.

"Tony," she said, "You need to reach Gabriella. She should know what these people are up to, what happened at the airport. She'd be expecting you in Rome." She put her hand on mine. "About Frank. Try her cell."

I was a little surprised, but pleased that Sonja wanted me to tell Gabriella about the FBI and my run-in with Pasquale.

"I left her a message last night, when I was in Paris. I haven't heard back."

"Call again. It's midnight here, six or seven in Rome; maybe you can catch her alone."

I had been hesitant to tell Gabriella too much. If she thought a relationship with her was threatening to me, she might back off.

I called. The phone was ringing.

"Is that you, Anthony? I was so worried when I got your message. Are you all right? Where are you?"

"I'm fine. I'm in Palm Beach." I thought it unwise to mention Sonja was listening.

"Are you alone?" There was a pause. "Can you tell me what happened?"

I didn't want to lie, or alert Sonja to Gabriella's concern. I ignored the first question. I told her about the message on the plane, about Pasquale and Emily. I finished with. "Emily said this Pasquale works for the Corsican Mafia."

"They are very bad people, Anthony. You are fortunate to have escaped. I am so glad you are safe. I loved seeing you on the plane, but it is better you are not here." She hesitated. "You know about my father. I'm sorry I had to keep that from you."

I expected more detail. When none came I said, "Frank is in the hospital in a coma; he may not live. It appears someone tried to kill him. Maybe Ryan."

This time her response was immediate and sincere. "Anthony! I am so sorry. He is your best friend, like a father. I am so sad for you." Her voice was kind, her words sympathetic, but I sensed a touch of underlying anger. "Get some sleep, Anthony. I will call you tomorrow."

Sonja, who had heard the conversation said, "It was wise not to tell her about me. She'd never believe I was on your side."

"I know," I checked my watch. "I need some sleep."

# Chapter 45

When you're overtired, sleep doesn't always come easily. Mine finally did, but it was restless sleep. I woke hourly, twice with dreams of Frank's funeral. A little after six, I got up.

The hospital switchboard connected me to Frank's floor. The grandmotherly nurse answered, "Oh yes, Mr. Tauck. No change in his condition. This type of trauma can take awhile. The day nurse is Evelyn Nesbit, ask for her."

"Thank you. You have been very kind." Working Intensive Care, what a job I thought, dealing daily with life, death, and the multiple emotions of friends and relatives.

"Have you spoken with Mr. Forbes' daughters?"

"Yes, they'll be here today, with the grandchildren."

I sleepwalked to the lobby and poured a cup of coffee. I hoped to run into my friend the valet, see if he'd heard from Ryan. No luck. After two cups and a scanning of the Palm Beach Post, I decide to take a walk.

I needed to confront Gabriella about Vitorio's death and her position of power in the Family. Could I be the lover of a Mafia don or donnette, whatever the term is? Sure. Could I be the husband? Not sure. Then I thought again about what she had said on the plane. Something she had told me on our first night together.

Walking blocks in a daze with no concept of time, I found myself in front of Green's.

I took a seat at the near-empty counter next to Linda, who works the cash register. As usual she and Nancy were laughing and joking about some local headline. I wondered where the church-goers were, and then remembered it was Monday. As I sipped my coffee the tone of Gabriella's voice, when I told her about Frank, came back to me. A low controlled anger. She sounded like she'd wanted to say something, but didn't. What else did she know she wasn't telling me? When would I see her again?

At that moment Gabriella phoned. "Anthony, how's Frank?"

"No change. Where are you?"

"Rome."

"When are you coming back?"

"That's why we need to talk. You need to know that my feelings for you are real. Three years ago my father financed Ryan's plan to buy policies. It was a business investment, all on the up and up. I discovered Ryan had corrupted it and I needed your help to understand what exactly he was up to. I never planned to fall in love with you, but I did. I miss you more than you can know, but it will be some time before I can return."

I felt a sense of panic. I was trying to process what she was saying, but only felt the fear of losing her. "Then I will come to Rome."

"No, that is not possible. You must understand I have commitments to my family and promises I made to my father that I am obligated to fulfill. It could take some time, perhaps a long time."

"But I must see you."

"Anthony, understand me. Our relationship is not ending; we just can't be together right now."

"Come to Palm Beach when you finish your business."

"No. You know from what happened to you at the airport that it is too dangerous, and I won't jeopardize your well being by involving you in my life. Please understand. We will still love, but only in our minds and our hearts until a safer time." The line went dead.

Nancy was watching me. "I heard your friend Frank had an accident. Nice man, hope he's OK."

I nodded, unable to speak or respond with more than a wave of the hand. I started out into the warm morning lost in my thoughts, tracing and retracing the events of the last few days looking for something I could have done to make things turn out differently. Was I on the verge of losing the two people I loved most? Then I realized that I had never asked Gabriella about Ryan and George.

I shut off my phone and started back to my hotel. I had lost at love before, but never when we both wanted it to last. Would I see her in six months, a year, five years? Would she meet someone else and forget me?

As I passed the wide driveway to the Breakers Hotel I realized someone was calling to me, blowing the horn. It was Mimi the medicine woman.

"My God, what is the matter? I've been blowing my horn and yelling till my lungs are sore. You look like you're sleepwalking."

I leaned my elbows on the open window of her Land Rover. "Sorry, I guess I didn't hear you. I'm not having a great day."

"Get in. I don't just dispense nutritional advice, you know."

I hopped in and started with Frank's being in a coma. Then, other than a few heated details, told her about Gabriella ending with her last words: "We will still love, but only in our minds and hearts until a safer time."

Mimi had parked across from the Brazilian Court and was listening intently. "You know Anthony, I've spent many years in Europe." She hesitated, and crooked her finger in that way she does. "Have you read nineteenth-century literature or seen the movie *Doctor Zhivago*?"

"Of course."

"Well so has Gabriella. I suspect she was raised on classical literature. While young women in this country were learning romance from soap operas, where women flit from bed to bed, Gabriella was reading about love that burned for years, through wars, revolutions, family tragedies. Only at the end of the story does the heroine meet or just miss the man she has loved and waited for. For Gabriella, loving from afar is romantic and very natural."

She sat for a minute, and then her tone changed from scolding to a resigned sadness. "How could you understand, Anthony? You're just another impatient twenty-first- century American male." I wondered if this wise woman had once been hurt by an impatient American male.

In fact I did understand. My Italian grandmother had planned to come to Boston to marry my grandfather, but when her mother became ill, she stayed to help with the younger children. It would be a long five years before she was able to come, marry my grandfather, and raise a family as originally planned.

"Thanks, Mimi, I think I understand."

I walked slowly to my room. Knowing Gabriella and I were reliving *Doctor Zhivago* made me feel less hurt. It was different, but it still hurt.

I took a hot shower and lay quietly on my bed. Sleep came quickly.

# Chapter 46

I was in grade school; a bell was ringing. Recess was ending; I had to go back to class. My feet wouldn't move. I woke in a panic. It was the phone.

"Tony, are you all right? You must have been exhausted. You're still asleep, and it's eleven o'clock." It was Sonja.

"No, I was up and went back to sleep. I spoke to Gabriella. It's not over between us but indefinitely postponed. Her family comes first."

"Tony," she was quiet for a long minute. "Oh Tony, I am so sorry. Do you have time to meet? There is something important I need to tell you. Can you be at Cucina by twelve?"

"Of course." The doubts and second-guessing about Gabriella and Frank resumed.

As I pulled up Sonja was talking to Nick, the oldest son in this family business. The family owns several places and they seem to have found the formula. Good food, attentive help, and a fun atmosphere keeps Cucina busy from breakfast through long after I care to be up. I parked across the street and ran across to her sidewalk table. I shook hands with Nick, who was just leaving, gave Sonja a kiss on the cheek, and sat.

She turned and held out her hands, palms up. I placed my palms against hers, not sure what was next. Her words were not what I expected. She squeezed my hands and said, "Tony, I phoned the hospital just before I called you. Frank passed away at nine-thirty this morning. I wanted to tell you in person."

"It can't be!" I struggled to stand, then sank back down. "I spoke to the nurse just this morning. He was stable."

People started to look over at me. I realized I was yelling.

"I'm sorry, it's true. I talked directly to the Intensive Care nurse."

I sagged deeper in my chair, placed my face in my hands and began to sob. I had shed tears at my mother's funeral, but couldn't remember my last real cry.

Embarrassed, I wiped my eyes with my napkin before picking up my head.

Sonja was studying the menu to give my feelings some privacy. "You know his children. They have been called, right?"

I nodded. "His daughters were called; they were coming to see him today."

I thought about the frayed photo of his grandchildren that he pulled out anytime he could get someone to look. I looked back at Sonja, who was watching me in silence. "I know he was almost eighty, but he had a lot left in the tank." I was suddenly so angry. "Tim Ryan has got to be involved. Has he been questioned?"

"We're looking for him now. He seems the obvious candidate, but we still need proof. Getting it may not be easy."

I suddenly felt overwhelmed with guilt. I had failed at balancing my reason for being in Palm Beach, to protect Frank, with my desire for Gabriella. "If only I'd been here, hadn't pursued Gabriella, this wouldn't have happened."

Sonja took my hand. "Don't torture yourself with those thoughts. Frank was his own man. Your being here wouldn't have changed things."

She looked up at the waiter. "Two Grey Goose martinis, straight up."

He nodded and turned away.

"You've had a tough morning, Tony. There's nothing either of us can do at this moment. You can find where his daughters are staying and meet them later."

I expected her to say something about Gabriella. She didn't, so I didn't. Best to put that away for now and deal with Frank, I thought.

We were into our third Grey Goose, and I was heavy into Frank stories. Sonja hadn't heard about his second wife, who loved to get undressed in the car, or just about anywhere else. She was nearly hysterical with laughter when I told her about his wife being drunk and naked in the passenger seat of his convertible when the state police saw her legs sticking out the window and pulled them over. Frank had thrown his jacket over her, but it only covered about half of her very well-built body. The state trooper's flashlight revealed more than he needed to see, or wanted to deal with.

"Oh! No!" was all he could get out. Then he smiled and waved him on with a "Drive carefully."

Wakes serve a wonderful purpose. They provide friends time to tell stories, remember the good times. Here we were, Sonja and I, drinking martinis and having our own little wake for our good pal Frank. Thoughts of Gabriella were laid to rest.

Later, when I thought about that afternoon I realized I had gone through all of Dr. Elizabeth Kubler-Ross's five stages of dying: denial, anger, bargaining, depression, and acceptance, and it had only taken four martinis. Finally, having been driven home by a friend of Sonja's, I lay on my bed and called Gabriella; she didn't answer. I left a semi-intelligible message, which included news of Frank's death, and something mumbled about Tim Ryan. It probably made no sense.

# Chapter 47

I woke late, ordered a pot of coffee and the newspaper in my room. The bell hop was at my door in moments. I propped a couple of pillows against the headboard and tried to make sense of the past week. Memories of Frank were interspersed with who really did what to whom, and why. Gabriella had said that Vitorio was only involved as a financial backer. But I was sure a man like that had to know the edge gained by owning insurance on unhealthy people. It was no stretch to picture Ryan, wanting to play the big shot, telling him the whole scheme. But how deeply was George involved? Who else? Gabriella must know, but she'd never reveal it.

In spite of three coffees, I fell back to sleep. I woke with a new energy and started picking up the clothes of the last few days, which I'd shed in heaps about the room. The jacket and tie I'd worn to Harriet's party were still in a heap behind the chair. Before putting my jacket in the laundry bag I checked the pockets and found two cards, Gabriella's and one other. I smiled at the memory and picked up the phone. "Hello Emile, it's Tony Tauck, we met at Harriet's par.."

Before I could finish he interrupted, "My God, how nice of you to call. My lunch date just cancelled, a gorgeous little coed here on spring break. Got cold feet. We were planning a trip to Wellington.

Have lunch, watch the polo matches, drink a little Champagne, then, who knows?"

He laughed, "Why don't you come along instead. I'm dying to worm the phone number out of you for that woman you met at Harriet's party."

"That might take more than a lunch, Emile, but I'd love to join you."

"Great, where are you?" I told him the Brazilian.

"I'll pick you up in front at 12:30 sharp, that'll get us there by one."

I looked again at his card, Emile DuPont. He seemed to know everyone in Palm Beach. I hoped that included Bingham, Burroughs and DuPont. A couple of hours with Emile would be a nice distraction and possibly fill in some blanks.

# Chapter 48

My valet friend and I were commenting on the better looks of the Jag vs. the 600 SL's better handling, but before I could ask where he was test driving my rentals, Emile arrived. His sapphire blue Bentley convertible settled the car dispute. I slid into the tanned leather seat, shook hands with Emile, and said, "This model can't hurt your dating."

"You like it? Silly question, what's not to like. Zero to one hundred in 5.1 seconds, all wheel drive, top speed 195. No it doesn't hurt my image with the girls I date, probably makes me look twenty years younger." He looked over and winked, "Which still doesn't bring us that close in age."

He was silent for a minute as he turned down Coconut and headed over the middle bridge. "I'm so glad you were available. These events are more fun with a compatriot with similar interests."

I laughed, "You just need someone to talk to the mothers while you spirit their daughters away."

I was trying to figure how to get the conversation around to Bingham Burroughs, when he asked, "Did you manage to steal that lovely woman from George?"

"You know George?" I said.

"Since he was a child. I don't advertise the fact, but we're partners."

I waited for more and Emile obliged.

"I'm listed as a senior partner in the firm, but these days I'm mainly active as an advisor and for my contacts, which through my family are extensive."

I decided to stay away from the DuPont connection, and said, "I can picture you as a good-will ambassador. Where did you go to law school?"

"University of Chicago."

I bit my tongue, waiting for some connection. It didn't come.

"I was working on my doctorate when my dad got ill and I had to come back and join the firm. He didn't trust anyone else to handle his clients. The firm was very dysfunctional at that time, a lot of senile old men handling the affairs of a lot of senile old men. We got it humming for awhile but the next generation has too many George Bingham types. The firm brings in very bright outsiders, but they can't deal with the familial issue. Partnerships outside the family are rare."

It seemed like the perfect opening. I said, "What's wrong with George?"

"If you gave him a brain he'd be on the floor playing with it." Then he added, "I also know, because I'm out and about, that he's involved with some very marginal people."

We had entered the club parking area. He got out of the car, tossed the keys to a valet who obviously knew him, and headed up the steps to the grandstand.

As we reached the top of the steps, two horses at full gallop were bearing down on the ball. The rider in red, closest to the sideline, had his stick raised for a neck shot to his teammate in front of the goal. His opponent in white was frantically spurring his pony to catch up.

Once settled in Emile's private box, I realized that, in spite of the visual created by the agility and speed of the players, it was my memory of the sounds of hoof beats that brought back the excitement unique to polo.

Emile, having participated in the sport as a younger man, was the perfect host. During a lull in play, he explained that the safety of the riders is the key objective of the two referees chasing the play. Penalty shots are given at various distances depending on the severity of the infraction and often determine the outcome of the match. I wanted to get him back on George, but there was too much going on. I thought, I'll ask again between chukkers, which are the seven-and-a-half minute periods of play.

As he spoke my eyes wandered to the other spectators in our section. The gentlemen in bright colored jackets and ties, the ladies all perfectly groomed, with straw hats, and their finest Tiffany pearls and Kaufman diamonds. Even in this section of beautiful people, one woman stood out. She was tall, slim, sitting with her hands folded on her lap, as though she were trained to the manners that a certain lifestyle requires. Her lips weren't full but somehow perfectly shaped as if created by nature, like a rose.

She must have felt my stare. She turned, our eyes met, and she gave me an innocent "How do you do?" smile. Maybe with all the emotion of the last two days it was only my imagination, but I saw a touch of sadness in her eyes that I remember to this day. Perhaps it was only a reflection of what she saw in mine.

Emile, always alert to the presence of a beautiful woman, said, "That is the countess Elizabeth Nadesca, reputed to be the most beautiful woman in South America. I have met her, she's very kind and unpretentious; quite an unusual woman."

I said, "Emile, the countess would be the most beautiful woman in any country she was in!"

By the sixth and last chukker we were finishing our second bottle of champagne. Emile's team in white was down six to five and his team's number two player was taking a mid-level penalty shot. Emile was standing at the rail yelling like a teenager. Behind me, I heard a soft voice with a strong Spanish accent. "Excuse me." I looked up and came face to face with the countess. She extended her hand, "I'm Elizabeth Nadesca. I don't want to interrupt Emile's concentration on the match. Would you give him this invitation?" I took her hand in mine and held it as long as I felt polite. Her fingers were long, her palm smooth and warm. Her hand and bare arm was absent any jewelry. Interesting I thought for a countess. I took the invitation from her other hand. She was smiling; that sadness had disappeared from the most beautiful dark blue eyes I've ever seen. For an instant, thoughts of Frank and Gabriella disappeared.

"I'm Anthony Tauck, very pleased to meet you. I will give Emile your note."

She started to turn away then stopped.

"You have suffered a loss, Mr. Tauck. I can see it in your eyes."

Surprised, I replied, "Yes, two close friends. One by death the other by circumstance."

She bent toward me softly placing her palm on the back of my hand.

"I too have had losses. Don't fight the grief. Allow it." She turned and was gone.

Emile's team had scored. The game would go into overtime. He sat down. I handed him the envelope. "From the countess."

"You met her?" he asked, stuffing the envelope in his jacket pocket.

"Yes, briefly." Then sensing time was short, I said, "Tell me about George Bingham, my competition. You said he was involved with some marginal people."

Emile turned to face me. The always present smile was gone. "I have a confession."

I must have looked confused because he finally smiled, "Nothing bad, it's just that I know who you are and what you are doing here in Palm Beach. I am a friend of Gabriella's, really her uncle's. I looked to meet you at the party. Her uncle has been a secret client of our firm for years."

"What? Why did you want to meet me? Because of her uncle?" I stammered.

"No," he said, "It's much simpler than that. Gabriella was trying to protect her uncle's reputation. I am trying to protect the firm. George Bingham and his cohorts were a threat to both."

I leaned back in my chair and rubbed my temple. "You both felt I could help, but Gabriella would be more, shall we say, persuasive."

He slapped me on the back. "Yes, and I'm sure you've been subjected to unimaginable torture."

I looked him straight in the eye and said, "Can I trust her?"

Emile shrugged. "I believe you can trust her, that is, within the confines of her objective, protecting her uncle's and her family's reputation." He paused, "Blood is thicker than water." Then added, "And of course she is a woman."

Driving back, I tried to ask him more, but he managed to avoid any details by responding in the same fashion that he had handled my, "Can I trust her?" If he knew of Vitorio's death, he didn't let on.

In the driveway of Brazilian Court we shook hands and planned to meet again. I thought about the fun-loving Emile I had first met, and the serious student who had once pursued his Doctorate in Law, hoping to teach. As Frank would say, "You can't tell a book by its cover."

# Chapter 49

Frank's funeral at St. Edward's was three days later. It drew a respectable crowd. A few old friends from Boston came down, but mainly Palm Beach people. Frank's friend, Barbara Mallory, threw a memorial reception at the Everglades Club. I even danced with her daughter Daisy. She was almost pleasant, and suggested I call her for lunch. I might.

Jennifer Maguire was there with her mother. We danced also, quite close, and agreed to meet soon for golf.

The grandchildren, whose frayed photos had become their grandfather's hallmark, were recognized and adored by everyone. Through them Frank's friends felt close to Frank. They smiled through tears at the many condolences.

I gave a speech about Frank's philosophy that ended with: "He never held back on the reins of life. He was respectful of other's feelings, but unconcerned about what people thought of him. He was unique." And he was.

Sonja and I were among the last to leave the reception. She was with Alex, who was thanking me for helping him with his job, when Sonja grabbed my arm and pulled me aside.

As we waited for the valet, she whispered "Tony, remember the body parts discovered on the beach we were thinking might be Mafia?"

"Ya. Through the pipes that dredge the channel. Weren't they identified?" I asked. Then looked at her, as if to say, why?

"Two vacationers walking the beach this morning at sunrise found new clothing and body parts strewn all over the beach. This time we didn't have to go to Italy to check the DNA."

Again, I gave her a puzzled look.

"Tony, it took no time at all to identify the bodies."

I flashed back to my conversation with Gabriella when I told her about Frank. Her tone had become so cold, and distant, that I had barely recognized her voice.

I started to laugh, perhaps not the normal way to respond, but somehow I knew.

She smiled and nodded. "Tim Ryan and George. Everyone is baffled as to who did it, and why."

Sonja stepped toward her car, and then turned back.

I mouthed the word, "Gabriella."

She smiled again, but this time only shrugged. "Case closed."

Violence begets violence. As glad as I was to have revenge exacted, it will never replace my loss. Revenge only feels good for a moment, the reason for wanting it lingers. I'd rather have Frank back!

# Chapter 50

Something kept me in Palm Beach, maybe memories of Frank, hopes that Gabriella would return, or just simple inertia. I thought about the words of the countess. "Don't fight the grief. Allow it." For several weeks I was pretty much alone with my thoughts.

Late one morning, I had picked up my coffee at Green's and was sitting by the beach reading the paper. An article by a female psychologist in Milan was expressing her views on Italian men, their mothers, their wives, and their mistresses. Like so many other prompts, it got me thinking about Gabriella. This time my realization of the vast difference in our cultures became more evident. I wondered if her grooming to be the head of a Mafia family had made her think like a man. If so, did she take on the male trait of seeking lust not love? Had our roles been reversed? What did love from afar mean to her?

As I gazed out at the reflected sun on the waves, I pictured Frank leaning back in his chair, his hands folded across his chest. He was explaining women.

"There are two approaches." He held up his index finger. "Commit yourself to one woman. But it must be the perfect fit, if not you risk getting hurt with a lot of emotional stress." Out came the second finger. "You can play the field with two, three, or more women. Here your greatest challenge is logistical. Little stress, little risk."

I nodded silently as he continued. "Remember, few matches are perfect. You will still need luck."

I thought about his comment that first night outside the Grill. *Suertes,* the moves the bullfighter uses to entice the bull, bring him close, excite the crowd, yet, remain unharmed. And *suerte,* the Spanish word for luck.

I thought about Gabriella far off in Milan. We had come so close. I knew some day we would meet again.

I thought about Mimi's comment, "You're just another impatient twenty-first century American male."

Then I thought about Daisy, and Jennifer, and Kate, and Sarah, and Grace May, all in Palm Beach.

I shrugged and pushed the speed dial.

"Dinner tonight at the Grill?"